Beginning Human Rights Law

Whether you're new to higher education, coming to legal study for the first time or just wondering what Human Rights Law is all about, **Beginning Human Rights Law** is the ideal introduction to help you hit the ground running. Starting with the basics and an overview of each topic, it will help you come to terms with the structure, themes and issues of the subject so that you can begin your Human Rights module with confidence.

Adopting a clear and simple approach with legal vocabulary explained in a detailed glossary, Howard Davis breaks the subject of Human Rights Law down using practical, everyday examples to make it understandable for anyone, whatever their background. Diagrams and flowcharts simplify complex issues, important cases are identified and explained and on-the-spot questions help you recognise potential issues or debates within the law so that you can contribute in classes with confidence.

Beginning Human Rights Law is an ideal first introduction to the subject for LLB, GDL or ILEX students and especially international students, those enrolled on distance-learning courses or on other degree programmes.

Dr Howard Davis is Reader in Law at Bournemouth University. As well as Human Rights Law he teaches Constitutional Law, Administrative Law and Civil Liberties on the University's LLB course and Constitutional and Administrative Law on the CPE/GDL course.

Publications include textbooks on human rights and civil liberties and articles on the Human Rights Act and its application in English law; his main research focus is on freedom of expression in a political context and the right to a fair hearing.

Beginning the Law

A new introductory series designed to help you master the basics and progress with confidence.

Published in Spring 2014:

Beginning Employment Law, James Marson
Beginning Evidence, Chanjit Singh Landa
Beginning Human Rights Law, Howard Davis

Also available:

Beginning Constitutional Law, Nick Howard
Beginning Contract Law, Chris Monaghan and Nicola Monaghan
Beginning Criminal Law, Claudia Carr and Maureen Johnson
Beginning Equity and Trusts, Mohamed Ramjohn

www.routledge.com/cw/beginningthelaw

Beginning Human Rights Law

HOWARD DAVIS

Routledge
Taylor & Francis Group

LONDON AND NEW YORK

First published 2014
by Routledge
2 Park Square, Milton Park, Abingdon, Oxon OX14 4RN

and by Routledge
711 Third Avenue, New York, NY 10017

Routledge is an imprint of the Taylor & Francis Group, an informa business

British Library Cataloguing in Publication Data
A catalogue record for this book is available from the British Library.

Library of Congress Cataloging in Publication Data
A catalog record for this book has been requested.

ISBN: 978–0–415–52464–3 (hbk)
ISBN: 978–0–415–52463–6 (pbk)
ISBN: 978–1–315–81536–7 (ebk)

Typeset in Vectora LH
by RefineCatch Limited, Bungay, Suffolk

MIX
Paper from responsible sources
FSC
www.fsc.org   FSC® C013056

Printed and bound in Great Britain by
TJ International Ltd, Padstow, Cornwall

Contents

Table of Cases

Table of Legislation

For Lydia and Edmund

Preface

Human rights is an important and interesting topic. Not a day passes but there is some story in the media dealing with human rights. Important political and social issues, such as the methods used to combat terrorism, the bullying use of social media, the concerns of celebrities for their privacy, the consequences for individuals of the advances in medicine, the use of surveillance by the state, and so on, all raise human rights issues.

Beginning Human Rights Law has been written to provide a brief introduction to the subject. It aims to introduce the basic principles of human rights law as these have developed under the European Convention on Human Rights and been given 'further effect' in United Kingdom law through the Human Rights Act 1998. The book explores the major issues and cases relating to specific rights and seeks to place these into context.

Chapter 1 introduces the topic as a subject for study. Chapters 2–4 explore the European Convention (ECHR) and the Human Rights Act (HRA). Chapters 5–10 then give consideration to specific rights – what they cover, how they have been given effect both in the Convention and in the UK law based on it, and what the main problems and issues associated with these rights are.

As well as text, throughout the book there are diagrams which clarify matters and there are also 'on-the-spot questions' of various kinds to stimulate reflection. Major cases are discussed and further reading is indicated at the end of each chapter.

The book aims, not at a detailed account of the law but, rather, to draw attention, in a straightforward and easy-to-read way, to the background ideas and the main purposes that lie behind particular rights – to the human interests that are served by these rules of law. Human rights are often controversial and so the book also aims to point out the main areas of disagreement.

With this bigger picture of what underlies the law, readers will be well placed to proceed to a fuller, more detailed study. There is a great danger of seeing human rights law as merely just another set of detailed, complicated, legal rules. Doing this may miss the moral and political seriousness which explains the special nature of human rights – that they should be legal limits on the exercise of power even in a democracy.

The author has taught, researched and written on human rights law (ECHR and HRA) at undergraduate and graduate level for a number of years.

The author expresses his sincere gratitude to Fiona Briden, Damian Mitchell and the rest of their team at Routledge for overseeing the preparation and production of this text; also for constructive and detailed feedback received at the beginning of the writing process.

Howard Davis
August 2013

Guide to the Companion Website

www.routledge.com/cw/beginningthelaw

Visit the *Beginning the Law* website to discover a comprehensive range of resources designed to enhance your learning experience.

Answers to on-the-spot questions
The author's suggested answers to the questions posed in the book.

Online glossary
Reinforce your legal vocabulary with our online glossary. You can find easy to remember definitions of all key terms, listed by chapter for each title in the *Beginning the Law* series.

Chapter 1
Introduction to the study of human rights law in the United Kingdom

LEARNING OBJECTIVES

On completing this chapter the reader should understand:

- The nature of human rights law in the UK
- The main sources of human rights law
- Some key points for answering human rights exam questions
- The name of some of the key printed and online resources relating to human rights law in the UK.

INTRODUCTION

Our understanding of human rights law can be helped by understanding the basic ethical or moral idea of human rights. Essentially, human rights are the entitlements of individuals which should be respected no matter who the individuals are or what they may have done. To deny a person their human rights is to refuse to treat them as a free human being, a full person in their own right.

These are basic entitlements which need the protection of the law. Therefore it is the responsibility of the nation states to protect human rights. But states, through their governments, are often responsible for rights being abused. Therefore, when states fail to protect human rights, it is important that there are also international remedies available. Indeed the standards of human rights law have been, to a great extent, set internationally (especially through the United Nations). The focus of this book is on the relation between, firstly, human rights at the European level (through the European Convention on Human Rights (ECHR)) and, secondly, on the way those rights are brought into UK domestic law through the Human Rights Act 1998 (HRA). You will need to be familiar with both the ECHR and the HRA.

Upholding person A's rights might involve undermining the rights of person B. If so, the right thing to do may be to limit A's rights. An example is where the media's right to freedom of expression may be restricted in order to protect a person's right to a fair trial – the laws of 'contempt of court' curtail the media's right to comment on a trial. In some, perhaps extreme, circumstances it may even be appropriate to curtail rights in order to protect a compelling general interest of the public. Judges applying human rights law are, therefore, often trying to balance rights with other rights and rights with other interests. As we shall see, one of the main jobs of courts dealing with human rights claims is to try and balance competing rights or balance rights with the public good.

The European Convention on Human Rights (ECHR) and the Human Rights Act 1998 (HRA)

The ECHR comes from the Council of Europe (not the European Union). It is a list of articles which embody basic civil and political rights, derived from the UN Declaration of 1948, and it is enforced by the European Court of Human Rights (ECtHR). Member states of the Council of Europe agree to ensure that their law and administrative practices are compatible with the ECHR. If not, individuals can go to the ECtHR, which is in Strasbourg, for a ruling. But the ECHR, because it is international law, is not directly enforceable in UK courts (see Chapter 2).

In simple terms, the HRA makes 'Convention rights' enforceable in UK courts. The HRA is an Act of the UK Parliament which, in essence, requires statutes to be interpreted, so far as possible, to be consistent with the rights in the ECHR and it makes it unlawful for government bodies and agencies (broadly defined) to do things which are inconsistent with those rights (see Chapter 3).

Protected Rights and Freedoms

So, what are the particular rights and freedoms which are protected through the ECHR and the HRA? This involves thinking about the underlying values which are being protected, the way the particular legal text which embodies the right has been interpreted, the way in which the legal right has been applied by the courts and the sort of impact on aspects of political, economic, social and private life it has had. Before doing this for particular rights you need to be aware of some of the general approaches taken by the ECtHR and the UK courts to the interpretation of the ECHR – remember all texts need to be interpreted but the rules and principles governing interpretation tend to be external to the text (see Chapter 4).

- A society that failed to outlaw intentional killing or which allowed torture would be one in which people are treated as mere physical objects to be disposed of at will and not as human beings. Articles 2 and 3 of the ECHR deal with these matters and we can see, in the text, interpretation and application of these articles, the seriousness with which these rights are taken (see Chapter 5).
- The same can be said for physical liberty. People who are imprisoned or otherwise locked up are no longer persons in the full sense because all their actions are controlled by their jailor. On the other hand, there are some very important reasons (punishing criminals is the obvious one) which can justify taking away someone's liberty. Article 5 ECHR deals with this and its point is to ensure that states only allow people to be imprisoned etc for good reasons and that these reasons are found in the law and their application to individuals can be tested by independent courts (see Chapter 6).
- The rule of law pervades the Convention (see Chapter 4). The basic idea of the rule of law is that people should only suffer disadvantage (such as loss of their

liberty or of their property) if this loss is a consequence of the application of pre-existing rules (laws). It would mean little, however, if people were not able to participate fully and equally in the various procedures (trials and other hearings etc) by which those legal rules are applied to them. This is the right to a fair hearing which is found in Article 6 ECHR (see Chapter 7).

- Totalitarian governments, such as the Nazis or the Stalinists, denied the humanity of their citizens by trying to control all aspects of life. A society which protects human rights, on the other hand, needs to recognise some 'space' in which the individual is sovereign and which the state cannot invade. This idea is found in the notions of 'privacy' (Article 8 ECHR) and 'property' (Article 1 of the First Protocol ECHR). But this is difficult and controversial territory. There are many situations in which a person may claim their privacy or property is invaded, but the state may also reasonably claim there are overwhelming reasons, based on the rights of others or the public interest, why this should be so. The need to deal with such dilemmas is found expressly in the text of both articles (Chapter 8).

- As well as having private lives we also have public lives. We live in a society subject to the law and government. We should not be merely subject to the will of those in power but should be able to participate in the way laws are chosen and be able to express ourselves on public affairs, not just because they may affect us personally but as an expression of our citizenship. Again, though, there are many situations in which such expression may restrict the rights of others or undermine the safety of others and so on. Articles 10 and 11 ECHR deal with these matters (Chapter 9).

- People have beliefs of various kinds, religious or otherwise, which may be central to their identity. Interference with these beliefs and the way they may be disclosed in public can be deeply hurtful and undermining of the sense of self. Again, though, showing belief, through dress or diet for instance, can be equally disruptive and disturbing for others. Article 9 and Article 2 of the First Protocol deal with this (Chapter 10).

BASIC STUDY SKILLS

Studying human rights law in the UK involves exploring both legislation and case law. You will need to become familiar with the HRA itself (it is a short statute and easy to read) as well as the ECHR, or at least its 'Section 1' (which contains the text of the rights outlined above). Likewise, major cases decided by the ECtHR, where they interpret the ECHR, need to be studied because UK courts must take these into account. Then, as regards UK law, you will need to demonstrate an understanding of the leading cases and apply the HRA in various situations. In this book the focus is on English and Welsh cases but there are also

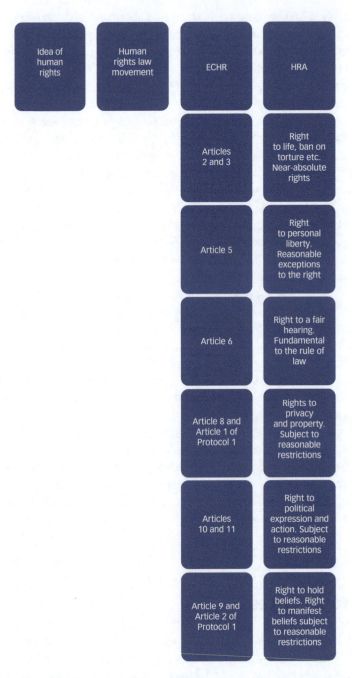

Figure 1.1 The development of human rights from idea to substantive law

some important cases decided in the Scottish and Northern Ireland courts. The focus is, therefore, on case law. The skill of reading a case involves:

- Getting a concise understanding of the important, relevant, facts. Reading the headnote of a reported case can help here.
- Understanding the legal issue in the case. In a human rights case the issue will usually be whether a particular action or decision of an official (civil servant, police officer etc) is compatible with human rights. This question will often involve an assessment of what is permitted by the terms of an Act of Parliament and whether what it permits is compatible with the rights in the Convention. It follows that you need to understand the legal context of the dispute.
- Noting the judges' analysis of the law – what is or is not permitted by Convention rights; and how this contributes to the outcome of the case.
- Understanding the reasons why the judges came to the conclusions they did – why they analysed Convention rights as they did. This is the important part for a student. The discussion about the meaning of Convention rights in the legal and factual context of the case is the part of the judgment to read most carefully.

SOURCES OF LAW

I. European law

In this context we mean the international law coming from the Council of Europe (not European Union law). The two main sources are the European Convention on Human Rights and the case law of the European Court of Human Rights.

The Convention is easily available. It is a good idea to bookmark the online Home Page of the European Court of Human Rights. The Convention can be found by clicking 'Basic Texts' from the left-hand menu. This will give you the up-to-date version (note that amendments and changes are made from time to time and it is not helpful to use an out-of-date text). Section 1 contains the substantive rights and Section 2 contains the rules concerning the ECtHR. (Note that Schedule 1 to the HRA also contains the text of most of the rights in Section 1.)

Likewise, the case law of the ECtHR is easily available. Click 'Basic Texts' on the left-hand menu on the Court's Home Page. This takes you to 'Decisions and Judgments' and then to HUDOC. HUDOC contains a comprehensive database of all the Court's judgments and a very wide selection of its decisions and reports on admissibility. It is a good idea to 'play' and learn how to use it. You can search for cases in all sorts of ways, such as the name of the applicant and respondent state or (useful if you are not certain of the name) by the application number. What is important is to make sure that you are searching for what you want. Note that the default setting will only search for 'judgments' on the merits of the case from a Chamber or Grand Chamber (which is what you are normally after). If, however, you want a 'decision' on admissibility, then go to the left-hand side of the screen and, under the heading 'ECHR Document Collections' make sure you click the box marked 'Decisions'. It is easy to forget this and so not find the material you are after.

How to read a ECtHR case

Since judgments of the ECtHR have to be taken into account by UK judges deciding cases under the HRA, you will need to become familiar with many of them. Judgments vary according to the facts and issues. But they seem, increasingly, to have a broadly common structure.

- The title page which gives you: the case name, the Section of the Court in which is situated the Chamber which decided the case; the application number; whether the case is a 'judgment' or a 'decision' (the latter is, normally, used in respect of admissibility); the date the judgment was promulgated (made public) and whether the judgment is 'final' or not – a decision is 'final' if the Grand Chamber is not going to be applied to for a rehearing (the decision of the Grand Chamber would then be 'final').
- The judges (normally 7; if there are 17 it means that the judgment is by the Grand Chamber) and the dates on which they deliberated.
- The procedure the court followed, under its Rules; there is also a list of the lawyers involved.
- The judgment then begins with the 'Facts'. These include

  o the circumstances of the case and the legal issues and the hearing of those issues in the domestic courts (applicants to the European Court of Human Rights must exhaust their domestic remedies first);

  o a discussion of the relevant domestic law and practice (but remember the ECtHR relies on how this is reported to it; it is not an authority on the meaning of UK law, for example);

  o a discussion of relevant international law materials if relevant (remember the ECtHR is an international court which can be influenced by broader international law);

  o the views of third party interveners (e.g. the pressure group Liberty) if they have been allowed.

- The judgment continues with the 'Law'. This means Convention law. It is the central, most important part of the judgment.

  o If there is an issue about admissibility (sometimes called a 'preliminary issue') then it will be dealt with here.

- The standard pattern is to consider the alleged violations article by article (if the violation of more than one article is alleged).
- The article dealt with is quoted.
- The submissions of the parties are stated and, to some extent, discussed. These are the submissions of the applicant, the government and any interveners.
- Then the 'Court's assessment'. This is the assessment of the issue and of the parties' arguments made by the ECtHR. It is the part that students should most closely focus on and read with greatest care. Normally the Court identifies the general principles concerning the article in issue and then it goes on to apply those principles to the facts of the case (hint: if you are trying to understand a case quickly, it can be sufficient to identify from the 'Facts' what the legal issue is and then go straight to the 'Court's assessment' and read the general principles part). At the end of the 'Court's assessment' there is a brief statement to the effect that the Court does or does not find there has been a violation.
- Remedies. The Court may then go on to consider 'the application of Article 41 of the Convention'. This deals with 'just satisfaction', which means financial remedies. Again, the parties may have made submissions on the point which are explained and then dealt with by the Court's assessment.

- The decision, on merits and just satisfaction is then summarised at the end of the judgment.
- The case is signed off by one of the Registrars.
- There may be some footnotes to the judgment.
- Dissenting judgments. These are allowed and can, over time, be influential.

Law reports and the ECtHR

HUDOC does not provide a full edited report. Fully edited reports give the reader the benefit of a headnote. This includes a summary of the facts, the main legal issues, the decision and the remedies. It can often help a great deal to get your bearings on a case by reading the headnote. Headnotes also refer the reader to the different paragraphs (or pages in earlier cases) where the points summarised are made in full. Where the report is carried online there will often be blue-text hyperlinks to cases and statutes and other materials referred to in the case. Law reports are not, unlike HUDOC, free and so your access to them may depend on your access to a library (carrying hard copy) or whether your university or college has a licence from one of the big law internet sites.

Two important series of such reports dealing with cases decided by the ECtHR are:

- The European Human Rights Reports – these are produced by Sweet and Maxwell, law libraries are likely to have hard copy and they are carried by

Westlaw UK; they are cited: *Pretty v United Kingdom* (2002) 35 EHRR 1 – the year of the report, the volume number and the case number (prior to 2000 a page number was used).

- Butterworths Human Rights Cases – these are produced by Butterworths, law libraries may have hard copies and they are carried by Lexis®Library; they are cited: *Pretty v United Kingdom* (2002) 12 BHRC 149 – the year of the report, the volume number and page number.

In both series, references in the headnotes are to paragraph numbers in the judgment.

II. United Kingdom Law

The main statute is, of course, the Human Rights Act 1998. This is widely available. As well as being found, as hard copy, in a law library (or, often, in a central public library) it can be downloaded using the official government's site: www.legislation.gov.uk/ (however, do note the warning that the version given may not contain amendments). The most reliable version, therefore, is again from one of the law databases such as Westlaw or Lexis®Library mentioned above.

The HRA allows Convention rights to be applied to UK law. Cases decided by UK courts dealing with human rights issues are reported in the ordinary law reports series – such as (mainly for England and Wales) the Law Reports (AC, QB, Fam, Ch), the Weekly Law Reports (WLR) and the All England Reports (All ER). These are in law libraries (hard copy) and also the Law Reports and the Weekly Law Reports are carried by Westlaw UK and the All England Reports by Lexis®Library. These fully edited law reports have keywords (to help searches for similar cases), headnote summaries which guide the reader to the decisive parts of the judgments and, if online, hyperlinks to the statutes and cases referred to.

These fully edited law reports are only available if you or, more realistically, your school, university or college library has bought a licence from the relevant publisher who owns the copyright. However case law and legislation is increasingly becoming available for free (there is arguably a human right, based on the rule of law, to free access to the law!). As mentioned above, statutes are available through 'legislation.gov.uk'. Case law is increasingly available through BAILII (British and Irish Legal Information Institute. This website (www.bailii.org/) hosts a wide range of judgments from many courts and tribunals and from different jurisdictions. Human rights cases in England are often decided by the Supreme Court, the Court of Appeal Civil Division or the Administrative Court (part of the Queens Bench) and, from variable start dates, these are easily found on BAILII. Supreme Court decisions can also be found, from the day they are promulgated, on the Supreme Court's website (www.supremecourt.gov.uk/).

ESSAYS AND PROBLEMS

Essay questions will usually involve testing both your general knowledge of a particular area of the law (e.g. the way an article in the ECHR has been applied in the UK, or one of the main provisions of the HRA) linked to some issue, controversy or problem concerning the way it is applied or interpreted. Thus it is testing both knowledge (particularly of ECtHR and UK case law) and also your ability to analyse and identify the underlying issue. After an introduction, the bulk of your answer should deal with making sure you give a full account of the law which is properly backed up by authority (case law) and demonstrates your understanding of the controversial issue in question. An important point is not to treat cases merely as outcomes (in which you simply say what was decided); try and discuss, instead, the reasoning – how the judges understood the law and why they understood the law in that way.

Problem questions involve applying human rights law to a situation posed in the question. When reading the quesiton about these given facts you will need to work out which articles, if any, are likely to be involved. For example, the question involves a police shooting, so think about Article 2 or Article 3; or the question involves a media story about a celebrity, so think about Articles 8 and 10. Assuming the question is about action taken in the UK you then have to think about why, in terms of the HRA, these articles should be relevant – usually because some public authority, such as the police or a media regulator is involved. Begin your answer by giving a clear account of those aspects of the law that are involved. Here you should discuss the general principles that emerge from the way articles in the ECHR have been interpreted by both the ECtHR and UK courts such as the Supreme Court (they are likely to be close to each other). Note that awareness of whether you are writing about human rights law at the international, European or UK domestic level is very important. Once you have given a clear account of the law, then you can apply it to the facts in the question. With problem questions it is usually important to give a clear account of the law first before applying it.

FURTHER READING

Websites

Websites (such as HUDOC, BAILII, Legislation.gov.uk., Westlaw and Lexis®Library) which carry relevant cases, case reports and legislation have been mentioned above.

Introductory texts

- Howard Davis, *Human Rights Law Directions,* 3rd edn, 2013, Oxford: OUP.

- Peter Halstead, *Unlocking Human Rights,* 2009, London: Hodder Education.
- David Hoffman and John Rowe, *Human Rights in the UK*, 3rd edn, 2010, Harlow: Pearson.

Major texts

Comprehensive account:

- Lester, Pannick and Herberg, *Human Rights Law and Practice* (carried on Lexis®Library).

On HRA in English law:

- M. Amos, *Human Rights Law,* 2006, Oxford: Hart.

On ECHR:

- Jacobs, White and Ovey, *The European Convention on Human Rights*, 5th edn, 2010, Oxford: OUP.
- A. Mowbray, *Cases and Materials on the European Convention on Human Rights*, 2001, London: Butterworths.
- D.J. Harris, M. O'Boyle and C. Warbrick, *Law of the European Convention on Human Rights*, 2nd edn, 2009, Oxford: OUP.

Civil liberties texts incorporating human rights law:

- Helen Fenwick, Kevin Kerrigan and Richard Glancey, *Q&A Civil Liberties and Human Rights,* 2007, Abingdon: Routledge Cavendish.
- Helen Fenwick, *Civil Liberties and Human Rights*, 4th edn, 2007, Abingdon: Routledge Cavendish.

COMPANION WEBSITE

Additional content from the author is available on the companion website:
www.routledge.com/cw/beginningthelaw

Chapter 2

The European Convention on Human Rights and its context

LEARNING OBJECTIVES

On completing this chapter the reader should understand:

- The idea of human rights and human rights law
- The international context of human rights law
- The Council of Europe and the European Convention on Human Rights (ECHR)
- The European Court of Human Rights (ECtHR)
- The impact of the Convention in the UK.

HUMAN RIGHTS

Definition

The moral or ethical idea behind human rights is that, in all we do, we should respect the basic humanity, the human dignity, of the persons affected by our decisions and actions. This is especially true for governments because they can use force in pursuit of legitimate social goals. 'Human rights' describe fundamental entitlements that flow from moral 'autonomy' (the sense of having consciousness and a capacity for choice) and the capacity for suffering that characterises each individual person. These can be distinguished from other more specific rights and duties (legal, cultural, ethnic, religious, sexual, moral, historical and so on) which distinguish us from each other. Human rights aim to answer the question: in what ways must others behave or not behave in order for someone to be treated as an individual human being in whatever he or she does or in whatever situation he or she may be in? A common way of putting it is to say that there is an inherent 'dignity' in all human beings which needs to be protected, and this is the purpose of human rights.

An important point is that human rights apply to human beings not because they are good or worthy, but because they are human. Human rights may, indeed, be important because they aim to reduce suffering but that is not the point. The decisive issue is that human rights are a necessary part of recognising that the being you are dealing with is a human. A difficult consequence of this is that even those who, for good reason, are unpopular or believed to be wicked, have human rights.

It follows from this that human rights may need to be upheld even in the face of common or social interests chosen in a democratic society. If 'democracy' means majority rule as expressed through representative institutions, then human rights are not 'democratic' (so most definitions of 'democracy' limit the idea of majority rule by various factors, including respect for human rights). This tension is reflected in the way rights are catalogued:

- 'Absolute rights'. Some human rights, such as the ban on torture, are held to be so fundamental that they can never be compromised or limited by arguments of the public good, no matter how strong.
- 'Limited rights'. Other human rights allow for certain defined situations in which they can be 'limited' in order to meet the normal and reasonable needs of a society (the most obvious example is imprisonment after conviction for a criminal offence which is a limit on the right to liberty).
- 'Qualified rights'. The exercise of these rights can interfere with legitimate social concerns or the rights of others (freedom of expression is an example). There needs to be scope for a 'balancing' exercise in which the impact of the individual exercising his or her human right can be measured against the consequences for the rights of others or significant public interests.

Of course, the identification and derivation of these entitlements of common person-hood takes us into the realms of philosophy and is various and controversial. For believers, basic rights have divine authority. Others, particularly in the eighteenth century, evoked the idea of human rights as 'self-evident truths' known through self-reflection and common reason. But in the twentieth century it was science that had intellectual authority and an evolutionary account of human nature perhaps explains human rights by disclosing an evolving tendency to compassion. A 'post-modern' perspective, on the other hand, rejects the whole idea of seeking a single general founding principle on which to explain the idea of human rights. So some philosophers take a different starting point. They ask what human rights is it agreed we have (as found in international treaties, domestic legal systems or common parlance, etc) and then identify the values that best explain and justify our having those rights. From this, for example, emerges the idea of individual 'autonomy'. We agree we have rights such as the right to life, not to be tortured, to freedom of expression etc. What explains these is a particular sense of being 'human'. Human beings are different from animals and from objects because they can reflect upon themselves and their conditions and decide for themselves the things that are valuable in life and what are reasonable ways of achieving these things. A human being loses her or his 'autonomy' and, therefore, is not treated as fully human, if others have complete control over them so that this ability of self-expression is lost. It is this sense of the basic conditions of individual humanity that, at root, human rights aim to protect.

Universal rights?

Human rights can be controversial. A major question is whether rights are really universal (apply to all humans) or whether they are culturally specific. It is sometimes argued that the idea of human rights, as it has developed in the last 50 years, is really an attempt to universalise 'western' conceptions of democracy and individualism (the individualism necessary for western consumer capitalism). The Organisation of African Unity, for instance, sponsors a charter of 'human and peoples' rights' which places an express emphasis on specifically African traditions and values and is unusual in having a section of 'duties'. Indeed there is a strong argument that it is such a regional approach to human rights, which can adapt human rights to history and culture, which offers the best protection. This book, for instance, is mainly about the European account of human rights.

Arguments of this kind need to be treated with care:

- traditions, after all, are both good and bad – Europe is formed as much by its wars and horrors as by its, rather later, traditions of democracy and law;
- arguments against 'human rights' on the grounds of cultural imperialism may function to protect tyrants and dictators from their critics and remove from victims a strong ground of support;
- in any case many specific human rights have considerable flexibility in the way they are applied – they can be adjusted to particular circumstances. The ECtHR, for instance, applies a 'magin of appreciation' under which it can give effect to human rights in ways which respect the cultures of different societies (subject to preserving the irreducible essence of the right).

On-the-spot question

 Make outline notes for a speech in which you discuss whether there is a real tension between human rights and democracy.

What rights do we have?

From a lawyer's point of view it is not necessary to try to answer this question philosophically. The lawyer can ask what entitlements have been agreed and expressed as rights (by legal systems, in international treaties etc). She or he can also ask what broad principles underly, explain and justify these agreed rights and whether, if those principles are to be applied equally and consistently, other specific rights ought to be agreed because they are implied by the underlying principles. The lawyer can also observe trends, observable amongst states, political parties and pressure groups, which may be pointing towards the recognition of other agreed rights.

It is helpful to make distinctions between various 'types' of rights, although, as always with typologies, there are significant areas of overlap.

- 'Civil rights' are the rights that developed in Europe and America from the seventeenth century. They embody the idea of the free man who is entitled to pursue his private life without oppressive restrictions imposed by state power and social status (such as was found in feudal society). From this idea of freedom comes, for instance, rights to bodily integrity (e.g. to life and not to be tortured), to equality under the law (including freedom of contract), to liberty (especially the right not to be imprisoned arbitrarily), to fair trials, to marriage and protection for private life.
- 'Political rights' are rights of the free person to participate in government. They include the right to vote and stand for public office and also the right of people to further their interests by seeking changes in the law and state practice through freedom of expression and freedom of association in political parties etc. These last two are also part of 'civil rights'. Historically 'political rights' have tended to come after civil rights (the main expansion of the franchise, the right of men to vote, in the UK was in the latter half of the nineteenth century; the political rights of women were not established until well into the twentieth century).

It is these civil and political rights that form the basis of the classic statements of 'human rights' written after the Second World War and found, in particular, in the European Convention on Human Rights.

But today the concept of human rights extends further.

- Equality rights. These are legally enforceable rights not to be treated less favourably on arbitrary grounds such as gender, race and, latterly, sexual orientation and disability. These rights tend to be focused on employment and the provision of services to the public. They also apply to the application of civil and political rights. In the UK women did not begin to approach civil, political and legal equality until the late nineteenth and early twentieth century (e.g. it was not until 1930 that all adult women got the vote).
- Welfare rights. These express the importance of education, health and welfare of various kinds by seeing them as basic rights.
- 'Third generation' rights: a range of other important human interests being put forward as subjects of fundamental and human rights. Environmental rights and rights to social development are examples.

Human Rights Law – national, international and regional levels

Protecting human rights requires something stronger than moral force. The primary way to do that is through the law and the state. Laws protecting human rights can be found at different 'levels' and it is important, at all times, to be aware of the level and what its implications are.

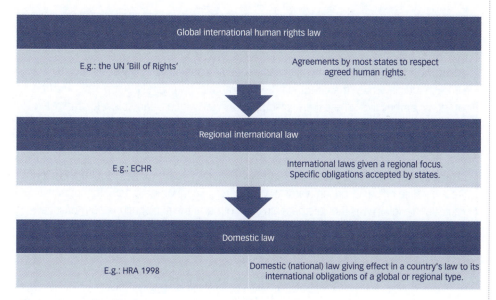

Figure 2.1 The different 'levels' of human rights law

To explain and illustrate the hierarchy of levels in the diagram, it is best to start
at the bottom, with domestic rights. This is where rights ought to be enforced but are
often not.

Domestic law

Nation states have primary responsibility for protecting human rights. National courts
have a duty to develop the national law, so far as they can, in ways that are compatible
with human rights norms. Of course this does not always happen. Domestic legal
systems, whilst effective and upholding the rule of law, are unable to develop adequate
protection of human rights norms (this was arguably the situation in the UK prior
to the HRA). More problematically, the legal system itself may be rotten. There may be no
rule of law but merely arbitrary government and widespread violence. Alternatively
there may be effective but wicked laws which embody state approval of the
widespread disregard of human rights norms (arguably the situation in South Africa
under apartheid laws).

A country's laws may protect human rights without there being express protection in
something called a 'human rights act' of 'bill of rights'. In England and Wales, for instance,
there is the common law's presumption in favour of liberty. This has found expression in
judicial remedies such as habeas corpus and the tort of false imprisonment.

> **Key Definition**
>
> **Common law:** These are the rules and underlying principles of law developed by the English judiciary over the centuries. The common law presumes that people are free to do what they like unless there is some other law which clearly prevents them. For instance, the common law has valued personal liberty and so laws restricting it (usually in Acts of Parliament) must be carefully scrutinised by the judges.
>
> **Habeas corpus:** An ancient common law remedy. English judges require a person (e.g. a police officer or prison warder) who is detaining another to bring that person to court and explain why they are detaining him or her. If the explanation does not satisfy the judges they must order the person's release.

Many western constitutional states have a long history of recognising human rights norms (perhaps expressed as liberties) in their own constitutions and laws. The French 'Declaration of the Rights of Man and of the Citizen' or the first eight amendments of the US Constitution are examples. But complacency is wrong. Such constitutions have been subject to suspension or ineffective application – failing to prevent the rise of Nazism, for example; nor did they guranteee equality for women, and the US Constitution tolerated slavery until 1865. Much European history honours human rights in the breach.

Global international law

The failure of some nation states to protect human rights has had to be remedied at the international level. Of course, international law is itself the creation of sovereign states or, at the least, involves their acceptance. Though partial international regard for some human rights norms has a long, if patchy, history, it was particularly after the horror and destruction of the Second World War that major states began to assume treaty obligations in respect of human rights. There is now a complex range of multi-lateral treaties by which states agree with many other states to accept various human rights as legal norms they must abide by. Major moments in this story include:

- 'International humanitarian laws of war': these are the laws flowing from attempts to ameliorate the consequences of war both for combatants and civilians. Their history can be traced back a long way (e.g. the ban by Pope Innocent II in 1139 of the use of the crossbow against Christians) but it is, in particular, the Geneva Conventions of 1949 with their additional protocols that form the basis of the modern law. These Conventions are supplemented by customary law which has developed over the centuries.

- *'International human rights law'* is a vast body of international law. At its heart is the United Nations, whose Charter was signed in 1945. The UN's purposes expressed in that Charter are wide ranging but they include 'promoting and encouraging human rights'. The UN's Declaration of Human Rights (adopted in 1948) sets out fundamental rights which states agree to support. It is not directly enforceable although can be of persuasive authority in international and domestic courts. After years of wrangling (the international context was the Cold War and a divided world) these rights were restated as legal obligations in two further treaties: the International Covenant on Civil and Political Rights (ICCPR) and the International Covenant on Cultural, Social and Economic Rights. These took effect in 1976. The three documents are collectively known as the 'UN Bill of Rights'. Since then many other treaties, focused on particular issues, have been adopted, usually under the auspices of the UN (e.g. to protect refugees and to eliminate racial discrimination and discrimination against women).

International human rights obligations need to be looked at carefully and they vary.

- ○ 'Soft' obligations may only require states to promote or aspire to an objective.
- ○ 'Hard' obligations require some system of enforcement. Usually the point of international law is that states agree to develop their domestic law so as to give an effective legal remedy in their national courts.

International institutions may be there to supervise the way in which 'hard' obligations have been given effect. State implementation under the ICCPR, for example, is monitored through states reporting every five years to the UN Human Rights Committee. The Committee then comments on these reports and in doing so can receive observations about the state's report made by interested NGOs such as Amnesty International or Human Rights Watch. If states fail to give full effect to human rights obligations there may be an individual remedy available at the international level, though, as with the ICCPR, this may depend on states agreeing to allow their citizens this right.

Customary international law complements the treaty-based law. Regarding human rights, this law derives from judicial and academic analysis of the legal standards that civilised states claim to stand for. These are then taken to be general standards to be upheld, in law, by all states whether or not they have specifically agreed to be so bound. Examples (and there are not many and the law is not clear) are the ban on torture and legal slavery. These rules can be known as *jus cogens* ('compelling law', the preremptory part of customary international law).

- There are other important international developments which relate to human rights but which are not fully under the auspices of the UN. Of particular importance is the International Criminal Court. It is established by international agreement under the Rome Statute. The Rome Statute defines in detail the offences of genocide, war crimes and crimes against humanity; the more controversial offence of 'aggression' (controversial because it might be used against 'western' powers undertaking actions such as the invasion of Iraq) might be added to the courts jurisdiction in the future.

Regional international law

The enforcement of international human rights law at the global level can be difficult. The remoteness of global institutions from the legal systems, societies, cultures and traditions of the states whose laws and practices their rulings concern can present major practical and political problems. As a result, a number of regional systems designed to protect human rights have developed. Africa, the Americas and the Islamic world all have their own charters of rights.

Perhaps the most influential is the European system. This is based around the European Convention on Human Rights, to which we now turn. The rights and freedoms catalogued in that Convention are given effect in UK law through the Human Rights Act 1998.

On-the-spot question

 Summarise the way in which legal protection of human rights is achieved – pay particular attention to the significance of the 'level' at which protection is available.

THE EUROPEAN CONVENTION ON HUMAN RIGHTS

The Council of Europe

The European Convention on Human Rights (ECHR) is an instrument of the Council of Europe. The Council of Europe is not anything directly to do with the European Union (EU) (though they share an anthem and a flag and, under the Treaty of Lisbon, the EU intends to sign up to the Convention).The Council of Europe was established at the end of the Second World War. Member states must base their law and practices on democratic principles and respect the rule of law and pluralism.

Key Definition

A society is pluralist in that, unlike a totalitarian society, its institutions are neutral on issues such as how individuals should live or what they should believe and, consequently, the laws allow people to express and organise themselves freely.

Until the collapse of the Communist bloc in the late 1980s, the membership was predominantly of western European states (Turkey was also a member from the beginning). These were countries which, after 1945, developed in similar ways. Their economic basis was capitalist, their institutions were reasonably open and democratic and their cultures were strongly influenced both by Christianity (the obvious exception being Turkey) and by the importance of individual liberty. These common features are important in explaining the success of the Council and the ECHR. From the 1990s, eastern European states including Russia, which were formerly communist, joined the Council of Europe and acceded to the ECHR. The development of those states into reasonable democracies has been the context of many cases brought under the Convention.

In 2013 there were 47 members of the Council. It works through a number of institutions, in particular the Committee of Ministers (made up of representatives of member state governments) and the Parliamentary Assembly (made up of representatives from the parliaments of member states). As well as human rights, it promotes its values over a wide range of areas (such as culture, education and health) and takes up world-wide causes such as the abolition of the death penalty, climate change and the protection of minorities. Unlike the EU, member states of the Coucil of Europe have not limited their sovereignty when they join. It cannot coerce its members through law. It works by persuasion and by demonstrating moral authority to the world.

The European Convention for the Protection of Human Rights and Fundamental Freedoms (the European Convention on Human Rights)

The ECHR was drafted by the Council of Europe in the late 1940s and came into effect in 1953. It has been added to since then by 'protocols' (14 in force in 2013, with 2 more open for signature). Section (or Part) 1 of the Convention is a statement of fundamental human rights whilst sections (or Parts) 2 and 3 establish and empower the European Court of Human Rights to deal with miscellaneous issues.

Under Article 1, signatory states agree to secure the rights and freedoms listed in the Convention. States, therefore, have the primary obligation to protect human rights. They must ensure that their laws and administrative practices provide for, and are consistent with, the Convention rights. They must also ensure that adequate, legal, remedies are available in the national courts for a person whose human rights have been breached (Article 13). If the national courts refuse or are legally unable to provide such a remedy, the state must permit individuals or organisations to send a case to the Court of Human Rights (Article 34). Under Articles 1 and 45, the states agree to accept and implement the judgments of the Court.

Article 1 also makes it clear that this protection is to apply to 'everyone' in a state. The Convention deals with 'human' rights, not the rights of citizens – because citizenship is a legal concept and states could (as the Nazi's did to the Jews) simply stipulate unpopular groups as non-citizens thereby removing them from the protection of the Convention. So everyone, even if they are convicted prisoners, unlawful entrants or over-stayers, 'paedophiles' or members of minorities who, rightly or wrongly are despised, etc, should enjoy these basic rights. The Convention also protects those, such as children and the vulnerable, who cannot claim protection for themselves. More problematically, 'everyone' includes corporations. This is made explicit in the right to property (Article 1 of the First Protocol) but nothing in the Convention prevents a corporation from enjoying any of the other rights which do not presuppose a physical body. Of course this is giving fundamental rights to bodies that may already have great economic power and which must act to maximise their profits. Much depends on context. There is a strong case that media companies, for example, should have rights of free expression. It is less clear, though, that international law should protect the property of commercial enterprises as a matter of fundamental rights.

Convention rights

The rights in the Convention take their inspiration from the civil and political rights in the UN Declaration of Human Rights. The UN Declaration also includes social and economic rights (such as a right to social security, to reasonable leisure and to a cultural life) which, with one exception (education) do not find expression in the Convention.

The Convention text of each individual right and the way that it has been read and given effect by the Court of Human Rights is all important.

- The rights are expressed in very abstract language and it is necessary to know what more particular and concrete rights and freedoms are covered (e.g. what is covered by the term 'private life' in Article 8 or the concept of a 'fair hearing' in Article 6).
- Although the main burden of each of the Convention rights is negative (defining things signatory states are not to do) the Court of Human Rights has frequently found that giving effect to the right must impose positive duties on signatory

states to do things. These can be free standing, but more often they are intertwined with negative obligations.

- Importantly, the text indicates the strength or weight of the right. Some rights are expressed in 'absolute' terms, others are 'limited' and others are 'qualified' (these terms have been defined above). These differences are critical to the way rights are interpreted and applied – particularly when weighted against other rights or the public interest.

The Convention also contains anciliary rights which deal with the way in which the Convention is to be applied (e.g. under Article 14 Convention rights must be applied without discrimination). These matters are discussed in Chapter 4.

The European Court of Human Rights

Rights without remedies are fairly useless. The strength of the Convention lies in the mechanism of enforcement and in particular the right of 'individual application'.

Key Definition

Individual application: Under the ECHR, states must allow their population to bring alleged violations of the Convention before the Court of Human Rights in Strasbourg. Member states agree to abide by the rulings and judgments of this Court.

At full strength the Court is made up of 47 judges, one for each signatory state. The aim is for there to be a reasonable gender balance and also for the different legal traditions in Europe (e.g. the common law and the 'civil law' traditions) to be represented. The Court's work is done by individual judges, by committees or by 'chambers'.

The two most important functions of the Court are:

- Admissibility. A case can only be decided if it meets a range of admissibility rules – for example, that effective domestic remedies have been exhausted and that there is a relevant, applicable, Convention right on which the applicant can rely. Most applications turn out to be inadmissible and it is individual judges or committees of judges that usually decide these matters.
- Judgment. In respect of admissible cases, the Court decides whether or not there has been a breach of the Convention. If it finds that there has been a breach, the Court can declare this and make a financial award (if it thinks it just to do so) and also award costs.

- Grand Chamber. There is no appeal but there can be a re-hearing before the Grand Chamber.
- Enforcement. It is the Committee of Ministers of the Council of Europe that has the final responsibility of monitoring compliance by the states of their obligation under Article 1 to give effect to judgments of the Court.

The Court has been very successful and, consequently, it has been overwhelmed by applications. There is a significant, though falling, backlog of cases (in 2013 this was about 120,000 cases). It has also been subject to some criticism particularly from those who think that it has interfered too much in the decisions and policies of reasonable democracies – that it has become a constitutional court for Europe rather than a reviewing court dealing with significant injustice (see, for example, Nicol 2005).

Major changes were made in 1998 (Protocol 11) to try and make the Court more efficient, but these have not succeeded. A reform process has resulted in a new Protocol (Protocol 15) being opened for signature in 2013 (it is unlikely to come into force for a number of years). Under the Protocol there will be more focus on the states providing better human rights protection and on the ECtHR being able to concentrate on the most serious cases.

The European Union: The UK is a member state of the European Union (EU). This is an organisation of states which is distinct from the Council of Europe. Unlike the ECHR, law made by the EU institutions can be directly enforceable in the courts of the member states. The EU is fully committed to human rights, including the rights in the ECHR. It has also developed its own Charter of Fundamental Rights which contains not only classic civil and political rights but also a fuller range of social and economic rights. The Charter has full legal effect on the EU's own institutions and applies to member states when they are giving effect to EU law. Charter rights are interpreted by the Court of Justice of the European Union whose judgments must be followed by the courts of member states. With the possible exception of some economic and social rights, the Charter is enforced in the UK.

On-the-spot question

 What is the Council of Europe, what does it do and how is it different from the European Union?

THE IMPACT OF THE ECHR ON UK LAW

The UK was one of the chief drafters of the Convention and the first country to sign and accept its obligations, although it was not until 1966 that the UK agreed to allow the right of individual application to its population. Generally speaking the UK has fulfilled its obligations in the sense of rectifying laws and administrative practices that the Strasbourg Court holds to be in breach of the Convention. Examples include:

- In 1987, the lack of detailed statutory regulation of telephone interception was held to breach Article 8 (respect for private life) – *Malone v United Kingdom* (1985) 7 EHRR 14. This resulted in the Interception of Communications Act 1987 (now the Regulation of Investigatory Powers Act 2000).
- The practice of dismissing homosexual service men and women from the armed forces was declared incompatible with Article 8 by the ECtHR in *Smith v UK* (2000) 20 EHRR 493 and, consequently, ended by the Ministry of Defence in 2000.

The UK's obligations under Article 1 ECHR continue to this day, despite the enactment of the Human Rights Act 1998. A recent example concerns the police database of DNA profiles which has been subject to more discriminating statute-based regulation following an adverse judgment from the ECtHR (*Marper v United Kingdom* (2009) 48 EHRR 50, followed by the Protection of Freedoms Act 2012, Part One).

The relationship of international and domestic law in the UK system is not, at all, an impenetrable separation. Quite the contrary. The UK's international, treaty-based, obligations have a strong, persuasive, influence on the courts in the UK and on the way in which they interpret statutes and develop the law. In particular the Convention has influenced the way in which UK law, specifically English common law, has developed.

Nevertheless, individuals were not able to enforce their Convention rights directly in UK courts. This was because UK law treats international and domestic law as separate systems (other countries allow for the integration of international and domestic law in a single system). The UK government may, through a treaty, commit itself to giving individuals certain rights. These rights can only have the force of law, be directly enforceable in the courts, if they are subsequently enacted in an Act of Parliament. And that is the point of the HRA. Without the HRA, Convention rights can only be directly enforced in the ECtHR in Strasbourg and that court's rulings do not effect UK law directly. With the HRA, Convention rights can be enforced in UK courts, though only in the particular ways allowed for in the Act.

SUMMARY

- Human rights refer to those basic entitlements that reflect our humanity and which are so fundamental they should have the support of the law.
- Consequently, human rights have been embodied in law at the international, regional and national (domestic) level.

- At the European level the European Convention on Human Rights provides human rights protection throughout the area of the Council of Europe.
- Although the Convention is not directly enforceable in the UK (though it is now given 'further effect' through the HRA, discussed in Chapter 3), it has had a considerable influence on the law and administrative practices.

ISSUES TO THINK ABOUT FURTHER

In thinking about the matters raised in this chapter, reflect upon the tension between human rights and democracy. What is it about a matter that makes it of such significance that it should limit what even fully democratic governments can do? Does the Convention contain too many rights that limit what democracies can do, too few or is it about right?

FURTHER READING

- Griffin, J., *On Human Rights*, 2008, Oxford: OUP.
  This is a learned and interesting philosophical discussion of the idea of human rights.
- Smith, R., *Text and Materials on International Human Rights*, 3rd edn, 2013, Abingdon: Routledge.
  This is a very useful compilation of text and materials on international human rights – looking at both the system and also at a range of particular rights.
- www.coe.int/lportal/web/coe-portal
  This is the website of the Council of Europe which is a comprehensive resource on all the activities of the Council, and includes everything you need for a study of the Court of Human Rights and access to 'HUDOC' the case law of the Court.
- Jacobs, White and Ovey, *The European Convention on Human Rights*, 5th edn, 2010, Oxford: OUP, Part 1.
  A first rate text book giving (in Part 1) a full discussion of the Court.
- Nicol, Danny (2005) 'Original Intent and the European Convention on Human Rights' *Public Law*, Spring, 152–172.
  This article (referred to above) discusses some of the criticisms about the ECtHR.

COMPANION WEBSITE

Additional content from the author is available on the companion website: www.routledge.com/cw/beginningthelaw

Chapter 3
The Human Rights Act

LEARNING OBJECTIVES

On completing this chapter the reader should understand:

- The reasons for enactment of the Human Rights Act (HRA) 1998
- The extent to which rights under the HRA will 'mirror' those available from Strasbourg
- The impact of the HRA on the 'separation of powers' in the UK constitution
- The nature of the duty, in s 3, to interpret legislation compatibly with Convention rights
- The nature of the duty, in s 6, on public authorities
- The role of Parliament in the HRA.

INTRODUCTION

The Human Rights Act 1998 gives 'further effect' in UK law to the 'Convention rights' found in the European Convention on Human Rights (ECHR). It does this in two ways, which should always be borne in mind.

- It requires, unless this is not possible, Acts of Parliament to be so interpreted that they can only authorise actions that are compatible with, consistent with, the human rights found in the ECHR (the 'Convention rights').
- It places a legally enforceable duty on public authorities only to act in ways which are compatible with Convention rights.

REASONS FOR ENACTMENT

The road to Strasbourg

The principal reason for enacting the HRA was to make available in UK courts the rights in the ECHR. Before the Act these 'Convention rights' were not part of the law of the UK. They were, though, influencing the way the law was developing and British people were bringing alleged violations before the European Court of Human Rights (ECtHR), often with success. Many thought it unfair that a person had to take his or her case to Strasbourg when UK law failed to provide an adequate remedy for a breach of human rights. Pressure from academics, politicians and senior members of the judiciary developed during the 1990s leading to some form of incorporation of the Convention being adopted by the Labour Party. The Party came to power in 1997 and enacted the legislation as part of a raft of other constitutional measures (such as devolution).

Constitutional weakness

Behind this there was also a sense that the UK was falling behind international human rights standards. In some areas, including police powers, public order and the protection of privacy, UK practices, whilst not oppressive by some international standards, disclosed serious weaknesses. Partly this sense came from particular events (such as the aggressive policing of the miners' strike in 1984–85). But it also reflected a more general critique of the UK constitution – particularly the legal sovereignty of a Parliament dominated by the executive (the Prime Minister and his ministers).

This point needs careful qualification. The English legal system (with equivalents in Scotland) already provided significant protection for individuals against arbitrary state power. The rule of law was well established and enforced by an independent judiciary. The right to sue the police for 'false imprisonment', the availability of 'habeas corpus' (which requires the courts to release a person unlawfully detained) and the power of the courts to set aside government decisions taken by unfair procedures, were already well entrenched in the judge-made common law long before 1998. Likewise political struggle, eventually expressed in Parliamentary votes, has given legal force to important rights, such as the right of women to vote; again, long before the HRA came along.

Of course, neither the judicial nor the Parliamentary record is always good. The common law did little to help women get the vote and Parliament, in times of perceived threats to national security, has often enacted draconian legislation undermining individual's rights. Nevertheless it is fair to say that most, if not all, rights in the ECHR already had some degree of existence, albeit incomplete and imperfect, in UK law before the HRA.

TYPES OF BILL OF RIGHTS

The problem in Britain was knowing how effective protection of human rights could fit into the UK's approach to democracy. Legal protection of human rights is done by judges. Judges in Britain are unelected, and there are good reasons for this. Nevertheless, human rights cases often involve protecting the rights of individuals or minorities against the wishes of the majority (as expressed in laws enacted by Parliament or decisions made by ministers accountable to Parliament). It can seem undemocratic. It was also necessary to ensure that human rights protection was consistent with the basics of the UK constitution.

Various versions were available:

- To give judges the ultimate power by allowing them to strike down valid legislation on the grounds of it being incompatible with human rights. The United States system is an example of this. Such a version was rejected for the UK because it was not consistent with Parliamentary sovereignty.
- To give the judges the power to invalidate legislation but make it subject to a legislative over-ride by which the legislature can re-enact the legislation the judges have struck down for a period of time (as in the Canadian system).
- To give the judges wide power of interpretation so that judges will give effect to legislation in human rights compliant ways if they possibly can – but there will be times when the legislation is so clear they will not be able to do this (New Zealand had a system like this at one time).

The UK's version, the HRA, has, as we shall see, aspects of the Canadian and the New Zealand approaches. The point is that, whatever version is chosen, some constitutional rebalancing between courts and Parliament is involved. The HRA does not, in the last instance, challenge the sovereignty of Parliament but it does introduce significant qualifications to that idea. Furthermore, it increases the influence of the courts in the general constitutional balance and the 'separation of powers'.

THE HRA: WHICH RIGHTS ARE INCLUDED?

The HRA does not 'incorporate' the ECHR into UK law because the ECtHR still does not have jurisdiction to determine directly the law of the UK.

What happens is this: the HRA defines the rights in the ECHR as 'Convention rights' and brings them into UK law by reproducing them in Schedule 1 of the Act. These are the traditional civil and political rights found in Part One of the ECHR along with the rights to property, education and voting found in the ECHR's Protocol 1; Protocol 13, which abolishes the death penalty, is also included. No new substantive rights are added nor are any subtracted. The same rights as the UK has signed up to in Strasbourg, but no others, are available for enforcement in UK courts under the terms of the HRA. Schedule 1 does not include the right to a remedy (Article 13) because it was considered that this right was satisfied by the HRA itself. Nor does Schedule 1 contain other substantive rights found in the ECHR, which the UK has not agreed to be bound by (such as the rights in Protocols 4 and 7).

THE STRASBOURG LINK

Section 2 HRA says that UK courts should 'take into account' the decisions of the Strasbourg Institutions (particularly the ECtHR) when deciding cases concerning the compatibility of UK laws and government practices with the Convention. This is different from the position of UK courts in European Union law, where they are required to follow (not just take into account) relevant decisions of the EU's Court of Justice. On its face, therefore, the HRA, unlike EU law, allows some divergence in interpretation of the Convention rights between UK courts in Strasbourg. In fact, though, UK courts have adopted a 'mirror' principle. They tend to the view that the authority given to them by the HRA is to uphold human rights in UK courts to the same or similar extent as those rights would be upheld by the ECtHR, no less but no further. There are a number of instances where the House of Lords/Supreme Court have made careful rulings on Convention rights that have then been found, by the ECtHR, to be providing too limited protection. The Strasbourg approach has then been accepted and followed by UK courts in later cases dealing with the same or similar subject matter.

KEY CASE: *Manchester City Council v Pinnock* [2010] UKSC 45

Background:

In *Qazi v Harrow LBC* [2003] UKHL 43, the House of Lords (the Supreme Court's predecessor) had held that a public landlord, with a clear legal right to evict a tenant, should be able to do so without the tenant being able to resist the eviction by claiming overriding Convention rights to private and family life based on Article 8. However, in a succession of cases, the ECtHR ruled otherwise – that, even when the right to evict was otherwise clear, a tenant's Article 8 rights might still need to be considered.

In the case MCC was a public landlord with a statutory right to evict P.

Principle established:

Eviction procedures before a County Court (involving a public landlord) had to allow for the possibility that the eviction should be stopped on the grounds of the tenant's Article 8 rights. There was clear Strasbourg jurisprudence on the point which needed to be followed and so *Qazi* was not followed (P's eviction was upheld on the facts, nevertheless).

But the issue is not straightforward. The Supreme Court held that UK courts should follow consistent, authoritative statements by Strasbourg of general principle ('clear and constant jurisprudence') concerning the application of a right, especially if from the Grand Chamber. But this does not necessarily apply if the Strasbourg case law is 'inconsistent with some fundamental substantive or procedural aspect of our law' or if it appears to overlook or misunderstand an important principle (*Pinnock*, para 48). Likewise the requirement to follow Strasbourg is less pressing when what is at stake is not an authoritative general principle of law but a particular application of the law to a set of facts. Here there is more room for manoeuvre and there may be 'special circumstances' why UK courts need not feel they have to follow the ECtHR.

The relationship with Strasbourg is a controversial one with some (including, in 2011, the Lord Chief Justice – Lord Judge, cited below) arguing that the UK courts, in particular the Supreme Court, should be more willing to have the last word on the law of the UK. Others would go further and want the UK to develop a more 'generous' approach to human rights. On this view the Convention, as interpreted by the ECtHR, is just the backstop, representing the bare minimum, and the HRA provides the opportunity for the UK courts and Parliament to develop higher standards of human rights protection than the Strasbourg court insists upon. Nothing in the HRA prevents this, but it is not the position currently adopted by the UK courts.

> ### On-the-spot question
>
> **?** Read Lord Bingham's judgment in *R (Animal Defenders International) v Secretary of State for Culture, Media and Sport* [2008] UKHL 15 – especially para 37 (just google the citation). Contrast his view on taking Strasbourg jurisprudence into account with Lord Scott's (paras 38–46). Which do you prefer?

THE HUMAN RIGHTS ACT AND LEGISLATION

The interpretative duty

Parliament makes the laws, the courts interpret and apply them. Acts of Parliament consist of general words and phrases and it is for the courts to apply these to particular situations. In doing so, they need to sort out any ambiguities and uncertainties in the language. The precise scope and meaning of an Act is often not clear and needs interpretation. Under the HRA, Acts of Parliament must be interpreted ('read and given effect') so that they can only authorise and permit actions, decisions, states of affairs etc that are consistent with the Convention rights in Schedule 1. But the HRA is quite clear. If, given the language of the statute, it is not 'possible' to interpret an Act in this way, the Act remains valid law, to be put into effect by the courts, even though it allows a state of affairs to exist which breaches an individual's human rights. The HRA does not give any court, even the UK Supreme Court, the power to invalidate, set aside or not apply a statute on the grounds that it breaches human rights – the USA's approach, mentioned above, is not followed.

The declaration of incompatibility

What the HRA does do, however, is to allow the senior courts of the UK to make a 'declaration of incompatibility' in respect of a legislative provision that it is not 'possible' to read and give effect to in a human rights compliant way. A declaration does not affect the law nor does it affect the position of the parties to the case – their human rights remain breached. The declaration makes the view of the courts clear (courts give full reasons for their decisions). It leaves the executive (government) and Parliament with choices to make.

- Do nothing. If so, a person who alleges their rights have been violated can still take her or his case to Strasbourg. If the person wins there, the UK government is under its treaty obligation (Article 1 ECHR) to take necessary steps to change the law in order to remedy the matter. Doing nothing, therefore, is likely to be merely putting off the day when the law must be changed to make it fit with human rights.
- Change the law in the normal way by using an Act of Parliament or using existing powers to change any offending secondary legislation. This is what usually happens.
- Change the law using a 'remedial order'. Section 10 HRA allows a minister to lay a 'remedial order' before Parliament. This order can, unless Parliament rejects it, change primary legislation. This is a controversial power since it comes close to allowing the executive to change primary legislation by order rather than by going through the procedures of an Act of Parliament. It can only be used where there are 'compelling reasons' that require a swift change in the law.

  Such orders can also be used to change the law following an adverse ruling from Strasbourg.

  Example: in *Gillan v UK* (2010) 50 EHRR 45 the ECtHR held that the lawful exercise by the police of powers of random stop and search under the Terrorism Act 2000 could violate Article 8. Using s 10 HRA the Home Secretary then suspended the operation of those powers. Later they were replaced by new, compatible, powers in the Protection of Freedoms Act 2012.

The HRA and Parliamentary supremacy

The idea that the HRA is consistent with the supremacy of Parliament is true but can give a misleading impression. The courts cannot invalidate an Act of Parliament but they can (as we shall see) subject it to radical interpretation. The alternative, a declaration of incompatibility, is highly likely to trigger an eventual change in the law. In effect, therefore, the differences between a fully fledged bill of rights (such as in the USA) where a supreme court can invalidate a statute, and the situation under the HRA, is much less than might be supposed. It may take longer but the eventual effects are similar.

The HRA is a major reason for thinking that there has been a rebalancing of the UK constitution by a shifting of influence in favour of the judiciary at the expense of the executive-lead Parliament. Where, under the traditional conception of Parliamentary sovereignty, the courts were clearly subordinate to Parliament, under the HRA the courts have a more decisive role when rights are in issue. Some commentators (e.g. Hickman, below) use the language of 'dialogue'. Under the dialogue theory:

- the courts, in their judgments, give reasons for why a measure is incompatible with Convention rights; then
- Parliament/executive 'reply' with reasons for keeping or changing the measure.

Supporters of this view are likely to expect the courts to make strong, uncompromising, statements of human rights standards, make declarations of incompatibility quite frequently but then leave it to the democratic institutions to face up to the issue and decide, clearly and deliberately, whether the political situation requires continuing with laws or policies which violate clearly stated rights.

An alternative theory focuses on the primary responsibility of the courts to secure human rights. Their job is not to rule on rights in the abstract but to apply rights in the circumstances that arise and rule decisively and finally, backing their rulings with a coercive remedy. If this means departing from the apparent will of Parliament, so be it; human rights are supposed to be binding on all state institutions, including the elected legislature. On this view, the courts should use their interpretative powers extensively and radically with the declaration being a last resort. It is a view which enhances the powers of an independent judiciary headed by the Supreme Court.

HRA: what is it 'possible' and 'not possible' for a court to do under s 3?

A difficult case under the HRA is one in which there is a statute which appears to authorise a breach of Convention rights. The job for the UK court is then to decide whether the statute can, nevertheless, be given a meaning, through interpretation, that prevents the breach or whether the right course of action is to accept that the Act requires or allows such breaches and make a declaration of incompatibility. The first course uses s 3, the second course uses s 4.

The basic principles were laid out in some of the early cases under the HRA.

KEY CASE: *Ghaidan v Godin Mendoza* [2004] UKHL 30

Background:

Under housing legislation a tenant's 'spouse' or a 'person living with the . . . tenant as husband or wife' could take over the tenancy on the tenant's death.

The question was whether the words in quotation marks could be read so as to include same-sex couples. This needed to be done in order to protect the Article 8 rights of such couples. The House of Lords said they could be so read.

Principle established:

- Prior to the HRA it was already the case that when a normal reading of an Act disclosed ambiguities and uncertainties these should be resolved in favour of a reading that made the legislation compatible with the Convention. This gave effect to the presumption, found in ordinary principles of statutory interpretation, that Parliament intends to legislate in line with the UK's international obligations, such as the ECHR.
- So s 3 only comes into play when the clear meaning of a statute is inconsistent with human rights.
- In such a case a court should be prepared to read-in a meaning to the statute which is consistent with the Convention; and do this even if it means stretching and straining the ordinary meaning of the language or reading-in words that are not there or ignoring words that are there. This is potentially a very radical approach and allows courts to go much further than, without the HRA, they are allowed to go.
- BUT: s 3 authorises interpretation but not legislation by the courts. What they can do, under s 3, must 'go with the grain' of the statute. It must not be inconsistent with the fundamental principles of the Act, even though it may alter some details. Their willingness to take such radical steps may also depend on the subject matter. Thus s 3 is more likely to be used if the legislation deals with matters that relate to the traditional concerns of the judiciary, such as fair trials or personal liberty, than if it concerns a matter of social policy on which the executive and Parliament are best informed.

If s 3 cannot be used to give a compatible reading, a declaration of incompatibility under s 4 may be used. Courts may choose to use s 4 rather than s 3 for various reasons including:

- that using s 3 would be constitutionally wrong in the sense that the judiciary would be usurping the clear intention of Parliament. Thus in *R (Anderson) v Secretary of State for the Home Department* [2002] UKHL 46 an Act of Parliament gave a role in deciding the length of prison sentences to the executive. This was inconsistent with the right to liberty in Article 5 of the Convention. The court made a declaration of incompatibility;
- that using s 3 would involve making a change that has major social implications which go well beyond the immediate issues in the case. The courts lack the competence to know of and assess the significance of these implications. Thus in *Bellinger v Bellinger* [2003] UKHL 21 the court refused to use s 3 in order to rewrite the law on marriage (the husband in a couple was a transsexual and the UK law insisted that a marriage must be between male and female).

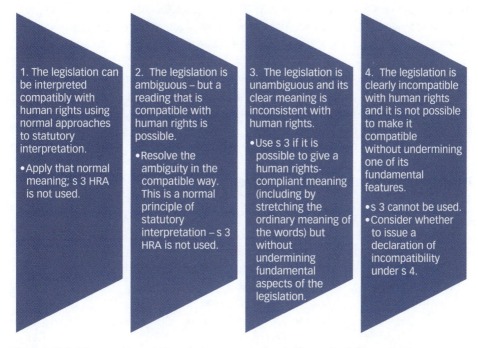

Figure 3.1 The matters taken into account by judges deciding whether to use the HRA

HRA: THE DUTY ON PUBLIC AUTHORITIES

The duty to act compatibly with human rights

The other major thing the HRA does is to place a legal obligation on a 'public authority' to act compatibly with the convention rights in Schedule 1 of the Act (s 6). Linked to this (ss 7 and 8) are procedures and remedies by which this duty can be enforced. Thus a person can seek a remedy against a public authority by bringing a case alleging a breach of human rights directly. Alternatively, a person can set up her or his Convention rights in any other proceedings – such as defending themselves in a criminal case on the grounds that evidence has been obtained in breach of Convention rights. The court can issue whatever remedy it thinks is appropriate, so long as it is within its powers. These can include a financial remedy (called 'just satisfaction'), which is not normally available as a remedy for an unlawful administrative act which does not involve a breach of human rights.

As we saw previously, it needs to be remembered that statutes that cannot be interpreted for compatibility with human rights remain valid and effective. Section 6(2), therefore, contains a proviso to the effect that a public authority which acts incompatibly with Convention rights because it is compelled to do this by an incompatible statute, will not be acting illegally. Parliamentary supremacy is also recognised by s 6(3)(a) which stipulates that Parliament is not a 'public authority' – there is no right of action in the courts against Parliament if it enacts legislation breaching human rights.

Human rights and private power

Section 6 reminds us that the primary duty to protect human rights lies with the state and its agencies and the HRA aims to make that principle effective in the UK. Private and corporate power, no matter how vast, is not directly bound by the Convention rights. However, private organisations may be subject to human rights in the following ways:

- The state may have 'positive duties' under the ECHR to ensure human rights are protected even in the private sphere.
- Section 6(3)(a) HRA makes it clear that courts and tribunals are public authorities. This can have implications for the way the common law, as it affects private individuals and companies and their rights, is developed.

An example of a private organisation in this context is a media company.

KEY CASE: *Campbell v Mirror Group Newspapers Ltd* [2004] UKHL 22

Background:

Photographs of Naomi Campbell coming out of a drug rehabilitation clinic were published in the *Daily Mirror*. The model sought damages for breach of confidence from the paper.

Principle established:

The traditional protection the law has given to confidential information can be extended to cover situations which may not be confidential, in the usual sense of the word, but are where a person has a reasonable expectation of privacy. This recognises the importance of a right to private life in Article 8. In the case this right needed to be balanced against the media's right to freedom of expression. A majority held that the balance came down in Naomi Campbell's favour.

What is a public authority?

The Act does not give a general definition of a public authority. The underlying idea is to allow actions in the UK courts against bodies for which the UK, as a state, would be responsible in Strasbourg. This includes the obvious state institutions such as civil service departments, local government and the police. But it is also clear that the state can be responsible at Strasbourg for private and semi-private bodies in so far as they act and take decisions which have an impact on individuals' human rights (in one case the UK was responsible for the use of corporal punishment by an independent school: *Costello-Roberts v United Kingdom* (1995) 19 EHRR 112).

The Act includes, as a public authority, 'any person certain of whose functions are functions of a public nature' (s 6(3)(b)). So the Act can impose obligations on:

- ministers, their departments and related civil service 'executive agencies',
- local government, and
- a vast range of 'non-departmental government organisations'. These exercise power at 'arms length' from ministers. An example is Ofcom which regulates broadcasting and telecommunications. Such bodies are 'public authorities' because they act solely in the public interest and have no other commercial or private side to their activities.

The Act can also apply to private individuals, commercial companies, charitable organisations, universities, schools, hospitals, professional bodies etc in so far as they are exercising public functions, even if they also undertake extensive private, commercial or charitable, activities. The point is to apply human rights to all bodies exercising public power (public functions). In the modern administrative world, this includes bodies which are also private, commercial or charitable. A security firm which also operates prisons under contract with the Prison Service, is an example.

What makes a function 'public' is not defined in the Act. The judges have said that understanding of the term will develop on a case by case basis. A range of factors have been identified, although none of them are necessarily decisive. Factors suggesting that an organisation is exercising public functions include that:

- it acts on the basis of special statutory powers (e.g. powers to regulate others in respect of a particular matter – powers not enjoyed by people generally),
- it is subject to democratic accountability (e.g. to Parliament or a local council),
- it is publicly funded (though this is not decisive),
- it has a duty to act in the public interest,
- if it did not exist its actions would have to be performed by a government agency.

It must be stressed that none of these are in themselves decisive. It is a matter of weighing all the relevant factors in the context.

HRA in action: the 'welfare gap'

KEY CASE: *YL v Birmingham City Council* [2007] UKHL 27

Background:

YL was a resident in a commercial care home. Her care was publicly funded by the NHS and a local council. YL sought to show that she had Article 8 rights against the care home. She needed to show that, in looking after her, the care home was performing functions of a public nature.

Principle established:

A majority of the UKHL held that the care home was not exercising public functions. In the context there was a clear separation between arranging care (done by the local council) and providing care on the basis of a commercial contract with the council.

In *YL* and other cases the courts may have denied the protection of the Act to some very vulnerable people. These are people who are cared for at public expense but whose care is provided to them by a commercial or charitable body under contract with a public authority such as a local council. In modern Britain this is how publicly funded care is characteristically delivered. As *YL* shows, the courts have tended to hold that the commercial or charitable provider who is solely providing a place to live and some degree of care, is not exercising a public function and so is not directly bound by the HRA. The provider is just bound by their contract.

Critics have argued that a public function relates to all aspects of the provision of services for which the state has accepted responsibility, and so the specific way in which that responsibility is discharged is irrelevant. This position has, broadly, been supported by a minority of judges and by Parliament's Joint Committee on Human Rights.

As regards residential nursing homes, the law has been changed by statute to ensure that they are likely to be directly bound by the HRA.

Functional authorities and private acts

The definition of a public authority is subject to an important qualification. A body which exercises public functions but which is not governmental in the broad sense and which also has a commercial or private side to its activities, is not bound by Convention rights in respect of its 'private' acts (s 6(5)). What gives an act a private character is not defined. For example, a person who is evicted by a charitable housing association may allege that the association failed to give proper respect to their right to a home under Article 8 (see Chapter 8). To make the case they will have to show not only that the housing association is exercising a public function, but also that the individual decision to evict is not best understood as the 'private' act of a landlord enforcing a lease (see *R (Weaver) v London & Quadrant Housing Association* [2009] EWCA Civ 587).

On-the-spot question

? You are the editor of the student newspaper at a university. You want to run a critical story about some aspect of university policy. The Vice Chancellor threatens to discipline you if you do. Consider whether you could bring an action for breach of your right to freedom of expression, in Article 10 ECHR/HRA, against the university?

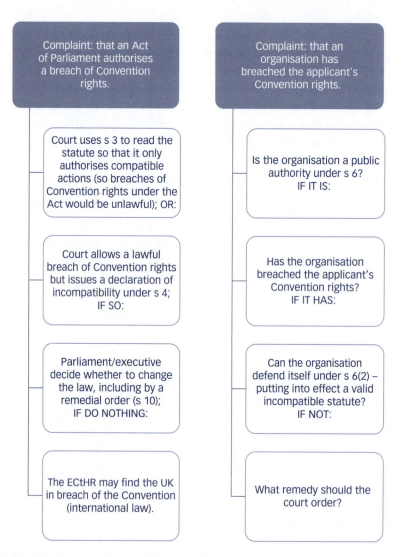

Figure 3.2 Summary of the main terms of the HRA

THE ROLE OF PARLIAMENT

Although the HRA focuses attention on the courts, the role of Parliament should not be forgotten. As said above, the HRA can be read as bringing about a form of dialogue between courts, Parliament and the executive on the proper way of protecting human rights. In particular, if the courts make a declaration of incompatibility, attention then switches to the executive (ministers) (who may suggest remedial changes to the law) and to Parliament (which must enact or approve these changes). If a minister decides to use a 'remedial order' (see above) then Sched 2 of the HRA lays down a procedure to be followed, which gives backbench and opposition MPs an opportunity to comment on and seek changes to the proposed order.

The importance of Parliament as an institution with responsibility for protecting human rights is also recognised in s 19 of the HRA. This requires a minister who is introducing a bill to make a written statement about the compatibility of its provisions with Convention rights. In the (very rare) instance that the minister does not think all the provisions are compatible, the statement must explain why, nevertheless, she or he wishes to proceed.

To assist its scrutiny of bills, Parliament has set up the Joint Committee on Human Rights. This surveys all bills before Parliament for compatibility with Convention rights, thus providing superb, detailed, advice to MPs. The committee also produces papers on general human rights themes aimed at informing debate (it is a great resource for students).

HUMAN RIGHTS CULTURE

One of the intentions behind the Act is to try to create a 'human rights culture' in the United Kingdom whereby the full range of public authorities and those providing public services would bring human rights considerations to the foreground and integrate them generally and self-consciously with the way in which they perform their functions. Some argued that the creation of this culture needed to be promoted by a taylor-made human rights commission. In the event the Equality and Human Rights Commission was created which seeks to integrate human rights promotion and monitoring with protecting, enforcing and promoting the wider law on equality and non-discrimination.

CRITICISM OF THE ACT

Many believe that the Human Rights Act has made an important, positive, difference to law and practice in the United Kingdom: that it has helped to ensure just treatment and a more generous society in which individuals are treated with more respect and more awareness of their individual circumstances and personal needs. But the Act has its critics who come from both the left and right of the political spectrum.

Some criticisms of the Act relate to its outcomes. Thus, it is sometimes seen as a measure that does little else but provide advantages for criminals and other undeserving groups. Often the examples given are simply wrong (prisoners do not have a right to pornography) or flow from an over-generous misunderstanding by officials of what the Act requires. In any case, the point is that a major aspect of the human rights idea is, indeed, the protection of unpopular minorities and individuals who are particularly vulnerable to oppression; to reject that is to reject the whole human rights idea.

Other criticisms go to the idea that the Act gives judges too much power at the expense of Parliament. This is answered by pointing out that, if this is the case, it derives from the wish of Parliament to limit its own powers in this way. On the other hand there are criticisms that the Act does not give judges enough power (because they cannot invalidate legislation) or that judges do not use the powers they have to the full extent allowed under the Act. Some such critics (Ewing and Than, below) point to how little judges have felt able to do, even with the Act, to protect those subject to serious restraint, such as under control orders. Others (Lord Judge, below), less critical, want to encourage UK judges to stand by their careful considerations of what human rights law requires and not automatically change them in later cases, just because the Strasbourg court has come to a different conclusion.

What is likely is that, within the next few years, there will be significant changes both at Strasbourg and domestically concerning the manner and form (and perhaps the substance) of human rights protection in the United Kingdom.

SUMMARY

The HRA enables individuals to pursue their rights under the ECHR in the courts of the UK.

The Act gives courts considerable freedom over the way they interpret statutes, but they must not use these powers to 'legislate', only to interpret.

Public authorities and other organisations exercising public functions must not violate peoples' Convention rights.

The other state institutions, ministers and Parliament, also have duties under the HRA.

ISSUES TO THINK ABOUT FURTHER

Conservative party policy (in 2010) was to repeal the HRA and replace it with a 'British Bill of Rights'. To that end a Commission on a Bill of Rights was established. It has produced a report discussing options on what this Bill of Rights would look like and how it might be different from the HRA. The report, 'The Choice Before Us' is worth thinking about. The Commission's website is www.justice.gov.uk/about/cbr.

FURTHER READING

- Lester, Pannick and Herberg, *Human Rights Law and Practice,* 2009, London: Butterworths (carried on Lexis®Library), Chapter 2.
  This is a full and comprehensive discussion of the Act.
- Joint Committee on Human Rights: www.parliament.uk/jchr.
  A superb resource. The Committee publishes reports on the human rights implications of Bills before Parliament and on general matters, such as the definition of public authority.
- Hickman, T., *Public Law after the Human Rights Act*, 2010, Oxford: Hart Publishing.
  A major analytical text on the effects of the Act.
- Kavanagh, A., *Constitutional Review under the UK Human Rights Act*, 2009, Cambridge: CUP.
  A major discussion of the constitutional implications of the Act.
- Ewing, K. and Than, J-C. 'The continuing futility of the Human Rights Act' (2008) *Public Law*, Winter, 668–93.
  A critical article which suggests that the Act has made little difference on important matters like the legislative response to terrorism.
- Lord Judge, Rt Hon. *Judicial Studies Board Lecture*, March 2010 (www.judiciary.gov.uk/ Media).
  An example of judicial concern about too close a relationship with Strasbourg.

COMPANION WEBSITE

Additional content from the author is available on the companion website:
www.routledge.com/cw/beginningthelaw

Chapter 4
Pervasive concepts and ancillary rights

LEARNING OBJECTIVES

On completion of this chapter the reader should understand:

- That a number of general concepts pervade the general understanding of the Convention, even though they are not expressly mentioned in the text; these include the margin of appreciation, the rule of law and the doctrine of proportionality
- That there are a number of ancillary rights which give individuals rights over how the main Convention rights are applied
- How the Convention deals with threats to democracy and human rights.

INTRODUCTION

Pervasive concepts

From Chapter 5 onwards the book considers the substantive law of the European Convention on Human Rights (ECHR) – the right to life, the right to freedom of expression, etc. The meaning, scope and application of these substantive rights is not obvious. The ECHR needs to be interpreted. In order to do this, courts, including the European Court of Human Rights (ECtHR), apply general principles which are not found in the text of the Convention. They are 'pervasive' in the sense that they apply throughout the Convention. These pervasive principles must be taken into account by UK courts when applying Convention rights under the Human Rights Act 1998 (HRA).

Ancillary rights

There are also a number of 'ancillary' rights in the Convention. These give individuals rights over the way in which the substantive rights are to be applied. Specifically, these are the right not to suffer discrimination in the way Convention rights are applied (Article 14) and the right to have a procedure and a remedy available from the domestic courts if there is a well-grounded allegation that a Convention right has been violated (Article 13).

Excluding rights

Under the Convention there are provisions which allow a state to limit people's rights. This can be in times of war or national crisis or when a person would use their rights in order to violate the rights of others. These two issues are discussed at the end of this chapter.

INTERPRETING THE CONVENTION

The Convention is a 'living instrument'

The ECHR itself does not say how it should be interpreted and applied. Therefore a theory about the point and purpose of the document is necessary. One approach would be to insist that constitutional documents should be interpreted in ways that give effect to the intentions of those who originally agreed or who subsequently amended it – but no further. In this way the ability of unelected judges to impose their values on society is minimised. Another approach, however, is to insist that constitutional documents need to evolve in order to retain their relevance and effectiveness in the society to which they relate. Although they should not impose their own values, it is part of their job to reflect the changing values of society in the way they interpret and apply the words in the document. It is this second approach that has been adopted by the ECtHR. Judges cannot amend the Convention (that can only be done by the state parties agreeing to 'protocols') but they can, and do, change its meaning and the way it applies in order to reflect their perception of social change. The Convention is a 'living instrument which . . . must be interpreted in the light of present-day conditions' (*Tyrer v United Kingdom* (1979–1980) 2 EHRR 1, para 31, and often repeated).

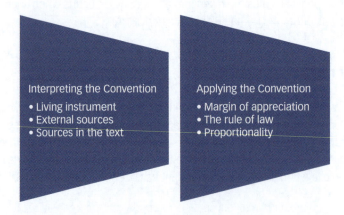

Interpreting the Convention

- Living instrument
- External sources
- Sources in the text

Applying the Convention

- Margin of appreciation
- The rule of law
- Proportionality

Figure 4.1 Summary of the pervasive principles of the ECtHR

On-the-spot question

Is it possible to have both national democracy and the Convention being interpreted and applied as a 'living instrument'?

International law

When trying to interpret and apply a difficult text, judges should still seek to apply the law, not their own views. They should look for some kind of legal authority to justify the approach they are taking. The ECHR is a treaty (a legal agreement between states) and there is a 'law of treaties'. An important element of this law of treaties is the Vienna Treaty 1969. This is a treaty dealing with the interpretation of treaties. It is a source of legal principles available to the Strasbourg judges seeking to interpret the ECHR. The Court's 'living instrument' concept, mentioned above, finds legal justification from the Vienna Treaty.

Other provisions of international law can also influence the way the ECtHR makes sense of its task. The UN Convention Against Torture, for instance, has been used by the Court in order to define 'torture' for the purposes of Article 3 ECHR.

Council of Europe sources

Closer to home, the Council of Europe (of which the ECtHR is a major institution) produces its own legal documents (such as other Conventions, Resolutions and Recommendations). These cover the wide range of issues with which it is involved. Again, the ECtHR can take these into account and be guided by them in the way it makes sense of the ECHR.

But it is crucial to remember that, in the end, the ECtHR's task is to make its own interpretation. It must not consider itself to be bound by these other external sources. They are no more than persuasive authority.

Interpretative sources internal to the Convention

In interpreting the Convention the ECtHR can also take account of internal textual matters like the title given to each article and also to other articles. Particularly noteworthy is the Preamble to the ECtHR. Although it does not confer any particular rights, it sets a democratic and pluralist 'tone' to the Convention which the ECtHR sometimes refers to when deciding issues about freedom of expression or association.

PERVASIVE CONCEPTS

Margin of appreciation

'Margin of appreciation' is a term widely found in international law and it has been of particular importance in establishing the authority and legitimacy of the ECtHR, even though it is not found in the text of the Convention.

In order to apply a Convention right in a specific situation, judgements may have to be made. For example rights to private life, manifestation of beliefs, speech or assembly (the rights guaranteed by Articles 8–11) can be restricted by laws or the action of state bodies, but only if the restrictions are 'necessary in a democratic society'. The 'necessity' for these restrictions is clearly a matter of judgement. Another example is Article 6. This guarantees the right to a 'fair' hearing. Obviously, whether a matter is 'fair' depends on judgement, it is not a matter that can be known with some kind of scientific certainty.

The question is then: who makes the judgement and decides what is fair or necessary? In the human rights context this is clearly a matter for the ECtHR. But the ECtHR might not always be best placed to make this judgement in particular cases. It may be reasonable to say that, sometimes, whether a matter is necessary or fair etc is best left to the national authorities, to the Parliament, courts or executives of the states. Then the job of the ECtHR is not to decide what was fair etc but, rather, to accept the decision of the state on the particular matter. The Court still has what it calls a 'reviewing role', it must ensure that the state, in any particular case, has not acted in a way that totally destroys the right in question. Margin of appreciation, therefore, allows rights to be applied in different ways in different countries; it does not allow the rights to be totally destroyed.

The idea behind the 'margin of appreciation' doctrine is that, on appropriate issues, the states are more closely in touch with the history, traditions and culture of their society and, therefore, better able to judge the need to interfere with or restrict the exercise of rights. It helps to reduce the kinds of tensions that can occur when an international court seems to be imposing its own values (or what it perceives to be generally accepted values) on a society which believes itself to be democratic and sees things differently. It also reflects the important point that it is the states who should protect human rights, the ECtHR stands behind as a guarantee.

But there is a danger. Too wide a margin can undermine the universal nature of human rights and the ability of the Convention to protect individuals and vulnerable groups. This is because, by applying a wide margin of appreciation, the rights of such groups become relative to the type of government and culture of the society in which they live. Therefore the margin of appreciation is applied in a flexible, issue sensitive, way:

- With absolute or unqualified rights then there may be little if any 'margin of appreciation' – there is no balancing of rights with public interests to be done and the ECtHR must apply its own definitions and understandings of the issue (whether police ill-treatment amounts to 'torture', for example, is for the Court alone to decide).

- With qualified rights (which require a 'fair balance' of individual and public interests) it may be that a wider margin of appreciation is allowed. But it is not automatic. Much depends on context and issue.

  - If the interference with a qualified right (such as the right to private life) touches matters that are personal and intimate, it may be that any margin of appreciation is narrow.
  - If the interference flows from the welfare policies adopted by the state, the Court may accept a wider margin of appreciation.
  - Where matters engage with controversial moral values and there is no consensus within Europe, the Court may allow a wide margin of appreciation.

Three examples indicate the operation of the doctrine.

KEY CASE: *Goodwin v United Kingdom* (2002) 35 EHRR 18

Background:

Goodwin, a transsexual, challenged UK law which prevented her changing her birth certificate to reflect her acquired gender.

Principle established:

Like the Convention, the margin of appreciation can evolve. Previous cases gave states a wide margin of appreciation over the legal position of transsexuals. But the ECtHR now changed its view. Medical knowledge and moral views throughout Europe had changed. States now had a duty under Article 8 to remove legal discrimination against transsexuals.

KEY CASE: *A, B and C v Ireland* (2011) 53 EHRR 13

Background:

Two women challenged Irish abortion law because it did not recognise dangers to the health or well-being of the mother as a ground for abortion.

Principle established:

The ECtHR can allow a wide margin of appreciation to states on moral issues. Views on abortion are highly controversial and the issue profoundly affects the moral beliefs of a society. Though unusually restrictive, Irish law, supported by its population, was still within that margin.

KEY CASE: *Hirst v United Kingdom* (2006) 42 EHRR 41

Background:

Hirst challenged the UK's blanket ban on convicted prisoners having the right to vote.

Principle established:

The margin of appreciation should not destroy the essence of a right. Article 3 of the First Protocol provides, by implication, an individual's right to vote (see Chapter 9). But this right is subject to reasonable restrictions and states have a wide margin of appreciation over what these restrictions might be. However, an unchallengeable blanket ban on voting was arbitrary and failed to protect the essence of the right. Therefore it was outside the margin of appreciation.

On-the-spot question

 In cases involving moral controversy (like abortion) is the ECtHR right to give a wide margin of appreciation to states, or is it really avoiding the issue and denying vulnerable women their rights?

'Law' and the rule of law

Another pervasive concept is the idea of law and the rule of law. A number of Convention rights expressly include the term. For example, interferences with a person's private life or freedom of expression etc can only be consistent with the Convention if 'prescribed by' or 'in accordance with' the 'law' (see Articles 8–11); likewise any procedure that leads to a person being deprived of his or her liberty (e.g. a criminal trial) must be 'prescribed by law'.

Any action by a state that interferes with a Convention right will be a breach of that right if it does not have a proper legal basis.

The important point is that the ECtHR has given the concept of law, as it applies to the Convention, its own particular meaning (it is an 'autonomous' concept).

- An action which interferes with a Convention right but which is also unlawful under the domestic law will breach the Convention. The ECtHR takes an inclusive approach to what counts as 'law'. Sources that are accepted as part of the law by the domestic courts will count as law from the ECtHR's point of view. Thus, in the UK 'the law' clearly includes Acts of Parliament, delegated (secondary) legislation and judicial decisions, but it can also include other sources, like Codes of Practice, which are accepted by the UK courts as having legal effects.
- This domestic law, however, must also satisfy further requirements of the Convention. It must be 'accessible' and 'foreseeable'.
  - 'Accessible' means that the particular rules of law that the state claims authorise the actions of its officials that are being complained about, can be identified directly or with legal advice. If no law covers the issue or if the legal authority on which the state relies is secret, there may be a breach of the Convention.
  - 'Foreseeable' means that the content of the legal rule in question must be sufficiently precise so that a person, or his or her advisor, can know whether what they are planning to do is likely to be covered by the legal rule. For example, those taking part in political demonstrations must be able to predict the kinds of actions that might trigger a police response. What is required will depend upon the context. If the state wishes to conduct secret surveillance which interferes with a person's private life, then the necessary powers need to be described in the law with some precision, whilst police powers over political demonstrations can be more loosely described.
- The domestic law must be non-arbitrary. The domestic law must be able only to authorise actions (by police etc) which are properly controlled and which make the authorities accountable for their actions and which give those affected sufficient safefuards. Laws which simply give the authorities wide and uncontrolled powers are likely to fall outside the Convention concept of 'law'.

An inadequate legal basis for state action, including inadequate legal protections for those affected, can often lead to a breach of a Convention right by a state. As ever, though, it can be very hard to lay down clear rules – what, exactly, is required by accessibility, foreseeability and non-arbitraryness depends on the general context and the specific situation.

Two examples affecting the United Kingdom:

KEY CASE: *Malone v United Kingdom* **(1985) 7 EHRR 14**

Background:

The High Court held that the tapping of M's telephone (in the context of a criminal prosecution) was not unlawful. At the time there were no UK laws which clearly authorised the phone tapping but neither were there laws that prohibited it. The High Court applied the common law rule that if something is not prohibited it is permitted. The ECtHR held that there was a breach of Article 8 ECHR.

Principle established:

Because telephone tapping represented an interference with a person's private life it needed proper legal regulation. The common law rule was insufficient – it did not provide proper procedures or adequate safeguards. (Following this case, legislation was introduced to regulate telephone tapping – see now the Regulation of Investigatory Powers Act 2000.)

KEY CASE: *R (Purdy) v Director of Public Prosecutions* **[2009] UKHL 45**

Background:

Mrs Purdy had a terminal illness. She wanted to know whether her husband would be prosecuted if he assisted her in dying at a time of her choice.

Principle established:

The fact that her husband might be prosecuted interfered with Mrs Purdy's right to respect for her private life. The legal basis for any decision to prosecute included the Code for Crown Prosecutors which the DPP followed. In relation to assisted suicide the Code did not meet the conditions of accessibility and foreseeability. The factors which prosecutors take into account needed to be made clear so that people in Mrs Purdy's position could make informed choices.

Proportionality

The term 'proportionality' is not in the Convention, but pervades it. The general problem of human rights law is that often an individual's right may conflict with the rights of others or the public interest (which may well involve the wealth, security and happiness of many). Sometimes rights 'trump' or outweigh the rights and interests of others. The right not to suffer torture and inhuman treatment etc (Art 3) is 'absolute' because it cannot be compromised no matter how pressing the rights and interests of others might be. More often, though, the language of a Convention right allows some degree of weighing up of the various interests affected. The Convention right is not merely one factor amongst others but the Convention text does allow for justified interferences. Similarly, the Convention right may use a term like 'fair' (e.g. Art 6 – the right to a 'fair trial') which inherently requires a weighing up of different factors. In particular, Articles 8–11 (respect for private life and freedoms of belief, expression, association and assembly) all allow interferences with those freedoms if they are 'necessary in a democatic society' in order to pursue a legitimate purpose (see Chapters 8, 9 and 10).

Fair balance

'Proportionality' is the idea that when the proper application of a right requires weighing the Convention right against other factors, the result should represent a 'fair balance' of all these factors. To repeat, this is not treating a person's right merely as one factor equal to others but it requires assessing whether, and to what extent, reasons for restricting the application of a Convention right, based on the rights of others or the social good, are justified.

Asessing the proportionality of an interference with a person's private life, or freedom of speech etc involves examining the detail of the particular situation that has come before a court. There are, though, various general reasons which point to an interference being disproportionate. For example, interferences based on applying inflexible, 'blanket', rules may suggest a lack of a fair balance and proportionality, because there is no room for exceptional cases or individual characteristics. Likewise, an interference may be thought disproportionate if there is a clear alternative way of achieving a legitimate purpose which has a lesser impact on the individual; or, again, if there is an interference without any attempt to provide safeguards and thus protect the minimum 'essence' of the right.

Deference

Proportionality is a matter to be decided by the courts (e.g. a UK court applying the HRA 1998 or the ECtHR).

For the ECtHR the question arises whether it should apply the margin of appreciation doctrine, discussed above.

For a domestic court a parallel question arises, should it 'defer' to the judgement of the executive or legislature. 'Deference' has been a very controversial doctrine – too much 'deference' can undermine the protection offered by human rights law. The courts have to identify and give weight to the range of competing factors in a case. Sometimes the proper thing to do is to accept the judgement of the executive or Parliament on some issue because, in the context, these bodies are better placed than the court to decide. For example:

- the interference with rights may derive from a complex issue, involving many different interests a court cannot assess;
- a public body may be a focus of expertise on a particular issue which the court does not have;
- the policy in issue was chosen by Parliament which is a democratic, elected, body.

But such issues might also touch on matters that are within the main concerns of the courts. A matter of national security (the responsibility of the executive) may involve depriving people of their liberty (a particular concern of the courts). Then the courts may feel it their duty not to defer to the minister's views but to decide for themselves, on the information before them, whether human rights have been violated. Where an alleged violation of a human right is based on the application of an Act of Parliament, the court must decide how much weight to give to the fact of Parliament's democratic legitimacy.

An example of different views on deference is:

KEY CASE: *R (Pro-Life Alliance) v BBC* [2003] UKHL 23

Background:

The BBC refused to broadcast a party election broadcast because it contained graphic images of abortions. Under its Charter and Licence (equivalent to statute) the BBC had a duty not to broadcast offensive matter. The political party objected that its right to freedom of expression had been violated.

Principle established:

The Court of Appeal characterised the BBC's actions as censorship at election time and found a breach of Article 10.

The majority of the House of Lords, on the other hand, felt it was not in any position to substitute its view on what was offensive for that of the BBC. The BBC had the duty and the experience on this matter to which the court should defer.

ANCILLIARY RIGHTS

Anti-discrimination: Article 14

Oppression of people, on the grounds of their race, gender or other aspects of their identity, has scarred European history; as have more subtle forms of limiting people's opportunities and experiences on such grounds. The second half of the twentieth century has seen a sustained attempt to use the law to eliminate it. This has occurred at the international level (e.g. the UN Convention to Eliminate Discrimination Against Women), at the national level (e.g. Race Relations Act 1976) and at the regional level – in particular initiatives by the European Union which EU member states are required to give effect to in domestic law. In the UK, for instance, the Equality Act 2010 provides a system of rights and remedies mainly aimed at discrimination in employment, the supply of services and the functions of public authorities such as local councils. But there is not a residual right not to suffer discrimination which is not covered by this or other specific Acts. Rather late in the day, the ECHR was added to by Protocol 12. This does grant a general right not to suffer discrimination in respect of 'any right set forth in law'. However, the UK has not agreed to be bound by Protocol 12.

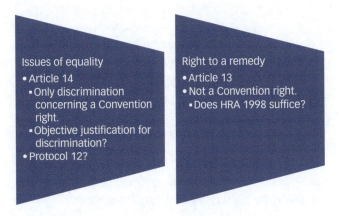

Figure 4.2 Outline of Articles 14 and 13

Article 14 ECHR (one of the original articles) has a limited role. It does not prohibit discrimination generally, but only in respect of the way the rights and freedoms guaranteed in the ECHR are put into effect. In order to show a breach of Article 14:

- It is not necessary to show that the law or government action, which is alleged to be discriminatory, involves a breach of a substantive Convention right. It is only necessary to show that the law or action is 'within the ambit' of such a Convention right (i.e. it relates to the subject matter covered by the substantive right). For example, suppose that laws dealing with marriage treat people differently on grounds of race, there could be a breach of Article 14 in relation to Article 12 (the right to marry) without there necessarily being a breach of Article 12.
- It is necessary to show that the alleged discrimination is on a ground recognised by the Convention. In fact the text of Article 14 is remarkably open. It refers to 'any ground such as sex, race, colour, language, religion, political or other opinion, national or social origin, association with a national minority, property, birth or other status'. The term 'other status' means that discrimination against homosexuals or persons of a certain age may raise an issue under Article 14.
- Not all discrimination (treating people differently) is bad. Differences in treatment, even on grounds of identity or status, can sometimes be justified. Where a difference has a 'reasonable and objective' justification there is no breach of Article 14. Differences in treatment which aim to correct previous disadvantage, for example, might be so justified. It is for a court to decide whether sufficient justification has been made out. Where there is at the heart of the difference in treatment a reasonable application of social policy, a court is unlikely to intervene (e.g. treating pensioners residing abroad less favourably than those living in the UK – *R (Carson) v Secretary of State for Work and Pensions* [2005] UKHL 37). But where, in a court's view, the difference in treatment reflects prejudices which should be redressed, it may find a violation (as in the unequal application of child maintainence arrangements to homosexual couples – *JM v United Kingdom* (2011) 53 EHRR 6).
- Sometime the issues that point to discrimination are also sufficient to show a breach of the substantive right. In such a case, a court may think it unnecessary to apply Article 14.

On-the-spot question

Consider Protocol 12 – do you think it should be brought into UK law or is it better to deal with equality issues by specific legislation?

The right to a remedy: Article 13

If a person has an arguable claim that one of their substantive human rights has been violated, Article 13 requires states to give a remedy. This means that there must be a fair legal procedure available through which the claim can be tested and, if proved, an adequate remedy provided.

Article 13 is not amongst the Convention rights in the HRA. The government felt that the HRA itself provided a sufficient remedy. In fact, however, there are a number of situations in which the adequacy and fairness of legal procedures to deal with alleged breaches of the Convention in the UK has been questioned. In the context of anti-terrorism law, for example, there are a number of 'special courts' which sit in secret and which do not allow full rights of participation (e.g. the Special Immigration Appeals Commission). Their procedures and remedies need to be sufficiently fair (not in breach of Art 6 at least) to avoid violating Article 13. Likewise, if the type of hearing and remedies available cannot deal properly with all the issues raised, Article 13 may be breached. In *Reynolds v UK* (2012) 55 EHRR 35, for instance, the lack of adequate legal remedies for death caused by negligent hospital care (in breach of Art 2) was a breach of Article 13.

SUSPENDING RIGHTS

'Derogation' in times of emergency: Article 15

Human rights apply even to those who are believed to pose a danger to the national security of the country. However, human rights theory and the liberalism on which it is based has always accepted that it might be necessary to limit rights in times of war or

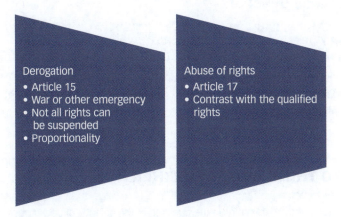

Figure 4.3 Outline of Articles 15 and 17

national emergency. Limiting rights is called 'derogation'. The ECHR allows this, but any such 'derogation' must be compatible with Article 15.

- There must be a 'war' or 'public emergency threatening the life of the nation'. The ECtHR grants a wide margin of appreciation to states on the question of whether such an emergency exists.
- Not all rights can be subject to derogation. Article 3 is one that must be guaranteed, even in wartime – war or public emergency cannot be used legally to excuse torture or inhuman treatment.
- Any derogation must be limited and proportionate to the needs of the situation. Famously the House of Lords held, in 2004, that detaining certain foreign terrorist suspects was inconsistent with Article 15: detention of foreign suspects was disproportionate because it left equally dangerous UK citizens still free (*A v Secretary of State for the Home Department* [2004] UKHL 56).

Prohibition of the abuse of rights: Article 17

The great dilemma of human rights theory (and of liberalism) is the extent to which those who would destroy human rights, and who seek to undermine an open, pluralist, society, can themselves enjoy human rights. Such people and organisations can have human rights (they should not be tortured or detained without trial and so on) but should not be allowed to use their rights in order to attack the rights and freedoms of others. This is the point of Article 17 – 'Prohibition of the abuse of rights of others'. Article 17 can be used, for instance, to prevent racists from asserting their rights to freedom of speech or extreme political parties from challenging legal bans. Article 17 is not often used. The same protection of democracy and the rights of others can be obtained by considering whether an interference with freedom of belief, expression or association is justified under the terms of the second paragraphs of Articles 9, 10 and 11 (see Chapters 9 and 10).

SUMMARY

Principles and values, such as the rule of law, margin of appreciation, proportionality and anti-discrimination, pervade the Convention. They are fundamentally important because they control and structure the way in which Convention rights are applied by the courts.

ISSUES TO THINK ABOUT FURTHER

Proportionality and deference raise the question of the balance of power between the courts and Parliament and the executive. How democracy and human rights relate together is an on-going and controversial matter that needs to be thought about.

FURTHER READING

- Hickman, T. *Public Law after the Human Rights Act*, 2010, Oxford: Hart Publishing: Chapters 5 and 6.
  These chapters offer a full and critical account of deference and proportionality.
- Kavanagh, A. *Constitutional Review under the Human Rights Act*, 2009, Cambridge: CUP, Part II.
  Kavanagh's discussion of deference and proportionality has significant differences from Hickman's.
- Legg, A., *The Margin of Appreciation in International Human Rights Law: Deference and Proportionality,* 2012, Oxford: OUP.
  A full discussion of these issues, both at the regional and international levels.

COMPANION WEBSITE

Additional content from the author is available on the companion website:
www.routledge.com/cw/beginningthelaw

Chapter 5
Life and physical integrity

LEARNING OBJECTIVES

On completing this chapter the reader should understand:

- The main terms of Articles 2 and 3 as Convention rights protecting physical integrity
- The importance of the 'procedural' obligation to mount an independent and effective investigation where breaches of either article are alleged
- The reach of both articles into unintended deaths or inhuman treatment for which the state is responsible
- Some of the key cases – decided both by the European Court of Human Rights and the UK courts acting under the Human Rights Act 1998.

INTRODUCTION

Without life there is no human dignity. The protection of life is fundamental to all human activity and flourishing. It follows that those in authority should perform their roles in a way that protects and respects people's lives.

Human dignity also means that everyone's physical integrity should be respected. People should not be treated like objects. For example, laws should ensure that people can only be touched with their consent; and when people legitimately lose their physical independence (e.g. when they are lawfully arrested) they should still be treated in ways which respect their physical integrity.

This chapter will explore the way these very basic ideas are given effect in the European Convention on Human Rights (ECHR) and, in the national law of the United Kingdom, through the Human Rights Act 1998 (HRA).

THE RIGHT TO LIFE (ARTICLE 2 ECHR)

Let us begin with the right to life. Any human rights instrument that did not require states to respect life would be unthinkable. The importance of 'life' is already recognised. The point of human rights law is to require states to protect the right to life that is already established in human custom and in religious or moral beliefs. The UN's **International Covenant on Civil and Political Rights** (ICCPR), for instance, says that 'Every human being has the inherent right to life'. Similarly the first sentence of Article 2 ECHR says – 'Everyone's right to life shall be protected by law'.

Article 2, therefore, imposes on states a range of negative and positive duties required to guarantee that the right to life is respected.

No intentional killing

Article 2 is explicit about these duties in one respect. The second sentence says that 'no one shall be deprived of his life intentionally . . .'. Thus states must have laws which define 'murder' and which provide the means by which it can be investigated, prosecuted and punished. In particular, state agents (such as police, security services and the military) must not intentionally kill, except in very limited circumstances which are discussed below.

Warfare, of course, involves intentional killing. As a general rule states cannot use lethal force (force intending to kill) just because the country is facing a state of emergency. Suspending or 'derogating' from rights, which is allowed if done consistently with Article 15, is not generally permissible for Article 2 (derogation is discussed in Chapter 4). However Article 15 does allow states to derogate from their duties under Article 2 if conducting a 'lawful' war (probably, today, a war sanctioned by the UN) and the fighting is conducted in accordance with the Geneva Convention and other international laws governing the conduct of military force.

Another form of intentional killing that states have used is capital punishment – the death penalty imposed by a court of law to punish the worst offences. Article 2, in the original Convention, expressly allowed for the death penalty which, in 1950, was still widely used. Since then, in Europe, the argument that the state should not be allowed to use death as a punishment for murder, no matter how terrible the crime and even if there is a deterrent value (hotly disputed), has prevailed. It is banned by Protocol 13.

The general duty

Article 2 involves much more than just a ban on intentional killing. The general duty, in the first sentence, requires states to ensure that the right to life is respected generally. There must be laws, organisations and judicial procedures by which not only the use of lethal force but, also, other dangerous activities, are properly controlled and regulated. The law must provide not only for appropriate offences, such as murder and manslaughter, by which perpetrators can be punished, but also for forms of civil actions by which victims can be compensated. There must be adequate police forces, prosecution services, courts, prisons etc to give effect to these laws. There must also be proper means for deaths to be investigated. Of the utmost importance is that these laws and procedures must be capable of being used against officials – members of the military, police officers and so on.

The use of lethal force

The general duty applies to the use by state agents of **lethal force**.

Key Definition

Lethal force

Force which, though not necessarily intended to kill, could have death as a forseeable consequence.

It is not difficult to think of situations in which the use of lethal force by the state may be necessary and its use excused or justified. These are recognised in the second section of Article 2 and police and the military can only exercise lethal force in accordance with it. Thus the use of lethal force will not violate Article 2 if:

- it is 'no more than is absolutely necessary' (this is a high standard which could be more testing than the 'reasonable force' test found in English law; in practice, however, there may be little difference), and is done only for one of the following reasons:
  - to defend a person from unlawful violence (this includes self-defence);
  - to effect a lawful arrest or to prevent the escape of a person lawfully detained;
  - in order to quell a riot or insurrection.

In all cases actions must be proportionate to the circumstances. Police cannot shoot someone just because they are escaping or rioting etc. The use of force must be necessary in relation to the particular facts and threats of the situation.

In *McCann v UK* the European Court of Human Rights (ECtHR) identified the major requirements when state agents use lethal force causing death.

KEY CASE: *McCann v United Kingdom* (1996) 21 EHRR 97

Background:

- UK soldiers followed an active IRA unit from Spain into Gibraltar. As the IRA unit was leaving Gibraltar the UK forces opened fire and killed them. No attempt to arrest was made.
- The soldiers acted on the belief, found later to be false, that the IRA unit had planted a bomb which they could detonate remotely.

Principle established:

- Where the 'absolute necessity' for the use of lethal force was based on a misunderstanding of the facts, there will not be a violation so long as the misunderstanding was honestly believed, for good reasons, to be valid at the time.
- Article 2 can be violated (as in this case) if the management and control of the operation is flawed (e.g. by communicating to the soldiers an exaggerated degree of certainty that the IRA unit had a bomb and by failing to arrest the unit as it entered Gibraltar).
- Article 2 requires a proper investigation into deaths for which the state is responsible. This is a matter of great importance which is discussed later.

Positive duties

It is wrong to confine Article 2 to the deliberate use of lethal force by the authorities. Under the general duty, in the first sentence, states have to take responsibility for keeping their population safe from many different threats to life. These may come from the state but also from non-state sources – such as criminals, angry demonstrators or commercial undertakings making profits from dangerous activities. Article 2 may also mean that states must protect individuals intent on suicide or self-harm. These are 'positive' duties because they require the state to take action, including the expenditure of resources.

Positive duties to individuals

Under Article 2 a duty can arise, imposing a legal duty on the state, to protect a particular individual who is subject to credible threats against his life. The famous Strasbourg case is *Osman v United Kingdom*.

KEY CASE: *Osman v United Kingdom* **(2000) 29 EHRR 245**

Background:

- A teacher made threats against a pupil with whom he had formed an infatuation.
- The police knew of the threats but did not take measures sufficient to prevent attacks by the teacher which injured the pupil and killed his father and others.

Principle established:

- Where officials (such as the police, the prison service or others with responsibility for individuals) know or ought to know of a specific and deadly threat against an individual, there is a duty under Article 2 to take appropriate steps to protect him or her.
- This is not, however, an absolute duty. It must not impose unreasonable demands on the authorities and so its scope depends upon circumstances and resources.
- The duty did not apply in the case since the police had no reason to know that lives were at risk.

Prisons and hospitals have similar duties (for which the state is responsible under the Convention) to protect those in their custody or care. This applies both when the threat comes from others but also from persons themselves.

In England (applying Article 2 via the HRA) *Rabone* provides a good example.

KEY CASE: *Rabone v Pennine Care NHS Trust* **[2012] UKSC 2**

Background:

- A hospital allowed a voluntary mental patient (i.e. someone not detained under the Mental Health Act 1983) to go home. Away from the hospital she committed suicide.
- Her parents alleged a breach of Article 2.

Principle established:

- A hospital had a legal duty to protect a patient who was a known suicide risk.
- This duty was based on Article 2 and so could be pursued by an action brought under s 7 of the HRA and was independent of a claim based on common law negligence.

This duty of the state to protect a person from a specific, known, risk may also need to be discharged by a court (remember, courts are 'public authorities' and bound to act compatibly with Convention rights under s 6 of the HRA). In *Venables v News Group Newspapers* [2001] Fam 430, for example, two notorious child murderers (who had themselves been children when they committed the murders) were subject to a death-threatening hate campaign. The court issued an **injunction** protecting the new identities and addresses they had assumed on release from prison.

Broader positive duties

Article 2 obliges states to protect their populations from dangerous activities and environments. Again, it is not an absolute duty but a requirement to take reasonable and appropriate steps in the circumstances. In particular, it is to ensure that these activities and environments are properly and effectively regulated. A good example is *Oneryildiz v Turkey*.

KEY CASE: *Oneryildiz v Turkey* (2005) 41 EHRR 20

Background:

- O lived in a slum near to a municipal refuse tip. An explosion caused the death of O's relatives.
- Legal action was taken against some of the responsible officials but not others; and compensation awarded to O was never paid. The ECtHR found that Article 2 had been breached.

Principle established:

- Article 2 was not confined to the use of lethal force by state agents, but also required states to take appropriate steps to safeguard people from dangerous activities, public or private, that threatened life.
- In particular, the state had to ensure that there was a proper legal framework to deter threats to life and these could include ensuring that those responsible were identified and, if appropriate, punished.

The 'procedural limb' – the duty to investigate

From its earliest cases (e.g. *McCann*, above) the ECtHR has stressed what it calls the 'procedural limb' of Article 2. This is a duty on states to properly investigate deaths for which they have responsibility.

The purpose of the investigation is:

- To enable victims or their relatives (called 'indirect victims') to know and understand what happened and who was responsible. This need to know is of great importance to victims in terms of being able to come to terms with what has happened and explains the increasing importance the United Nations has given to a 'victim's right to the truth'.
- To identify those responsible so that, if necessary, they can be punished.
- To learn lessons for the future.

To achieve these purposes the investigation must meet various standards. It must, for example, be instigated by the state, be fully independent, have adequate powers to obtain the necessary information and be able to compel people, such as the police, to attend and give evidence; in particular it must involve the family. A failure to achieve this can violate Article 2.

A good example is the case of Baha Mousa. He was an Iraqi who was beaten to death whilst in the custody of British troops in Iraq. Because the events took place in a British base the British courts, under the HRA, held that Article 2 applied. The investigation by the Military Police was found to lack independence and thoroughness; and the court martial, by which only one soldier was convicted, was focused on the offences rather than on disclosing what happened in detail. The resulting public inquiry and report, a major undertaking, satisfied the demands of Article 2. (The final report is http://www.bahamousainquiry.org/report/index.htm.)

On-the-spot question

 Explore (e.g. by a Google search) and comment on the various procedures by which deaths for which the state is responsible can be investigated in the UK. Examples are:

- the coroner system in the UK,
- the Independent Police Complaints Commission,
- investigations under the Inquiries Act 2005.

Euthanasia

Modern medical technology can keep people alive in situations they find intolerable. If they are unable to commit suicide they may want the assistance of someone close to them so that they can die with dignity at a time of their own choosing. But assisting someone to die is, in most European countries including the UK, a crime. The role of Article 2 was discussed in *Pretty*.

KEY CASE: *Pretty v United Kingdom* (2002) 35 EHRR 1

Background:

- Diane Pretty had a degenerative disease. She wished for the assistance of her husband so that she could die at a time of her own choosing. The Director of Public Prosecutions refused to guarantee that her husband would not be prosecuted for murder.

Principle established:

- Article 2, the right to life, does not bring with it a corresponding right to die. States have no obligation to make euthanasia legal.
- Conversely, however, the Court refused to rule on whether Article 2 required states to ban euthanasia.
- A ban on euthanasia did interfere with the patient's private life (and thus involve Article 8) but the interference was justifiable (Article 8 is discussed in Chapter 8).

Abortion

This is, perhaps, the most morally controversial subject there is. It involves the intentional termination of a pregnancy. The ECtHR has consistently refused to rule that a foetus is definitely a 'life' to be protected by Article 2. This is because there is no agreement between the European states as to when 'life' begins (see *Vo v France* (2005) 40 EHRR 12). States have a wide '**margin of appreciation**' (see Chapter 4) on this issue. Restrictive laws which prevent abortion, even when needed to save a mother's life, are likely to violate Article 2; likewise, restrictive laws can interfere with a mother's private life, thus engaging Article 8 and raising the issue of justification (see Chapter 8).

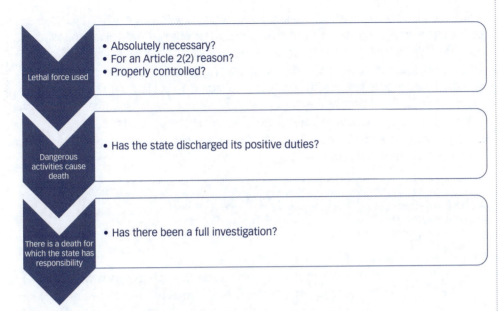

Figure 5.1 Summary of Article 2

THE RIGHT NOT TO BE TORTURED OR SUFFER INHUMAN OR DEGRADING TREATMENT OR PUNISHMENT (ARTICLE 3 ECHR)

Respect for physical integrity also involves the need for states to ensure that people are not physically or psychologically abused. This applies especially to those who are arrested, imprisoned or otherwise under the control of the state and its agents. Such people have no physical freedom and enjoy little if any capacity to make choices.

The kinds of behaviour that people need protection from is illustrated by *El-Masri v Macedonia* app 39630/09 Grand Chamber judgment of 13 December 2012, a case of 'extraordinary rendition'. E-M, a German citizen visiting Macedonia (Former Yugoslav Republic) was detained by Macedonian police at the border and held incommunicado for 23 days in an hotel. He was taken to an airport, handed over to the CIA, beaten up, stripped, a tranquillising suppository was forcibly inserted, he was dressed in a nappy, thrown onto an airplane and flown eventually to Afghanistan. At all times he was under the complete physical control of his Macedonian and CIA captors and everything was done outside the law. The ECtHR found that this was 'torture' and Macedonia had breached Article 3 ECHR by failing to protect him.

Article 3 is short and imperative: 'no one shall be subjected to torture or to inhuman or degrading treatment or punishment'. It is described as an 'absolute' right. It is unqualified: it does not allow for circumstances in which torture etc might be justified (compared with Article 2 which allows lethal force to defend others etc). Torture or inhuman treatment cannot be used to defend the rights of others or to promote a public good, nor is it excusable because it is used against people who are bad or dangerous. Further evidence of its absolute nature is that it is deliberately excluded from being a right that can be derogated from under the terms of Article 15. So war or public emergency cannot be used to justify torture or inhuman treatment.

KEY CASE: *Gäfgen v Germany* **(2011) 52 EHRR 1**

Background:

- Police had in their custody a man who, they strongly suspected, knew where a kidnapped child was being held. They threatened him with inhuman treatment. The suspect then disclosed the whereabouts of the child (who had already been murdered).
- The police officer was convicted of a criminal offence but only given a light sentence by the German courts.
- On a case brought by G the ECtHR held that the sentence was too light and so there was a breach of Article 3.

Principle established:

- Article 3 is absolute. The use or threat of torture by officials against those completely in their power is never justifiable, no matter how noble the cause, and how serious the wrongdoing.
- This needs to be reflected in the official responses to proven allegations.

On-the-spot question

Can torture ever be justified? In the USA there has been an extensive debate on whether if not 'torture' at least deliberate inhuman treatment of terrorist suspects can be justified. In favour are those who believe it is likely to produce evidence which, taken together, will allow the authorities to prevent other atrocities and save lives.

Against are those who believe that truth seldom emerges from such treatment and also those who uphold the moral imperative, reflected in Article 3, that treating people in this way is so inconsistent with their basic humanity that it can never be justified.

Threshold severity

Treatment only violates Article 3 if it crosses a threshold of severity. Treatment of lesser severity can engage Article 8 but it should be noted that the focus of Article 8 is on the protection of 'private life'; furthermore, an interference with an Article 8 right can be justified if it is proportionate.

Judgement on whether the treatment is sufficiently severe to engage Article 3 will depend upon the circumstances and on the ECtHR's sense of what is acceptable in Europe today. It may change with the times.

Torture

Torture is defined by the ECtHR as 'deliberate inhuman treatment causing very serious and cruel suffering'; this involves treatment which causes 'intense physical and mental suffering including acute psychiatric disturbance' (*Ireland v UK* (1979–80) 2 EHRR 25). As in *El-Masri*, the usual case of torture involves the direct or indirect approval of state officials; indeed the involvement of officials is part of the definition found in the UN Convention Against Torture (to which the ECtHR refers). Under the ECHR states must also ensure that torture by criminal gangs or private security organisations is illegal.

Torture has a special stigma. It engages the special revulsion of mankind. It is illegal under the domestic law of most (if not all) states. It is also illegal at international law with many countries signing up to the UN Convention, mentioned above. It is also banned by customary international law – law which is binding on states whether they have signed a treaty or not.

Torture evidence

The absolute nature of the illegality of torture (under the ECHR and international law) means that no one should be tried on the basis of evidence obtained by torture.

KEY CASE: *A v Secretary of State for the Home Department* [2005] UKHL 71

Background:

- Under the Anti-Terrorism Crime and Security Act 2001 foreign terrorist suspects could be imprisoned without trial. This was if they could not be deported because they might be killed or tortured in the country to which they were deported (Article 3 bans deportation in that situation).

- They could challenge the decision to deport them before a special tribunal: the Special Immigration Appeals Commission (SIAC).
- They argued that SIAC decisions were flawed because they might be based on evidence obtained by torture.

Principle established:

- Evidence that was obtained by torture was inadmissible in court. This was because torture evidence might well be unreliable but, even if reliable, it could not be admitted because to do so would be unconscionable (morally wrong).

Inhuman and degrading treatment or punishment

As mentioned above, treatment is 'inhuman' when, given a minimum level of severity, it involves actual bodily injury or intense physical or mental suffering. Where such suffering is deliberately imposed a court may have to decide whether to apply the special stigma of torture – as the ECtHR did in the *El-Masri* case mentioned above. This judgment will (like the issue of the general threshold of severity) reflect the ECtHR's view of changing European standards.

KEY CASE: *Ireland v United Kingdom* **(1979–80) 2 EHRR 25**

Background:

UK forces, as a matter of policy, subjected IRA detainees to hooding, noise, loss of sleep, reduced food and being made to stand in painful positions.

Principle established:

The Court of Human Rights held that this was 'inhuman treatment', not torture.

Nearly 30 years later:

KEY CASE: *Menesheva v Russia* (2007) 44 EHRR 56

Background:

M refused to allow Russian police into her boyfriends flat and was subjected to a serious beating, semi-strangling and threats of rape and harm to her family as a consequence.

Principle established:

The Court of Human Rights held, in the circumstances, this was torture.

Degrading treatment or punishment

These terms were defined in *Pretty* (above). Treatment or punishment is 'degrading' when it:

- 'humiliates or debases an individual showing lack of respect for or diminishing his or her human dignity', or where it
- 'arouses feelings of fear, anguish or inferiority capable of breaking an individuals moral and physical resistance'.

The scope of Article 3

Treatment by police etc

Adherance to Article 3 means that deliberate ill-treatment by officials (such as police abuse of a suspect or prison officers humiliating prisoners without good reason) should be subject to effective remedies under domestic laws. These should include, for the serious cases, prosecution and punishment under the criminal law. If necessary, domestic laws should also enable those affected to obtain damages or other civil remedies.

Lawful punishment

Article 3 also requires that the range of lawful punishments be consistent with the judicial view of what is inhuman or degrading. Corporal punishment for criminal offences was abolished decades ago in the United Kingdom and its incompatability with Article 3 was demonstrated in a case which led to the abolition of 'birching' on the Isle of Man (*Tyrer v United Kingdom* (1979–80) 2 EHRR 1). In the private sphere laws that allow 'reasonable chastisement' (e.g. of children by parents or teachers) must not be applied in a way that involves treatment (smacking, whacking, beating) above the Article 3 threshold of severity (which in the case of children is quite low).

Policy causing unintentional hardship

An important point about Article 3 is that it applies to 'treatment' or 'punishment' which is done (in a context for which the state has responsibility) for a perfectly lawful purpose but, as an unintended consequence, leaves a person in a condition which is inhuman or degrading. This can raise difficult questions in many policy areas such as:

- Medical ethics. In *Pretty* (above) the ECtHR accepted that medical action or inaction which left a patient in a situation which was inhuman or degrading could breach Article 3 even though the real cause was an illness, not any act by a doctor. The Court, though, emphatically, did not rule that bringing about the patient's death as the only means of avoiding the breach of Article 3, was thereby allowed.
- The treatment of prisoners. The Prison Service has to ensure that prisoners are not left in conditions above the threshold of severity. This can be important in respect of prisoners who are ill or who have disabilities – towards whom the Prison Service has special responsibilities.
- Welfare policy. Article 3 creates a minimum standard.

KEY CASE: *R (Limbuela) v Secretary of State for the Home Department* [2005] UKHL 66

Background:

- Asylum seekers, who had not claimed asylum immediately on reaching the UK, were banned from working and could not receive welfare benefits unless these were necessary, according to the Home Secretary, to prevent them suffering in breach of Article 3.
- Various claimants appealed against their denial of benefits.

Principle established:

- The court held that the Secretary of State had an absolute obligation to provide benefits to asylum seekers as soon as he became aware that his decisions may leave them in a situation where Article 3 would be breached.
- These claimants were denied the most basic human needs such as shelter and food. The threshold of severity was passed.

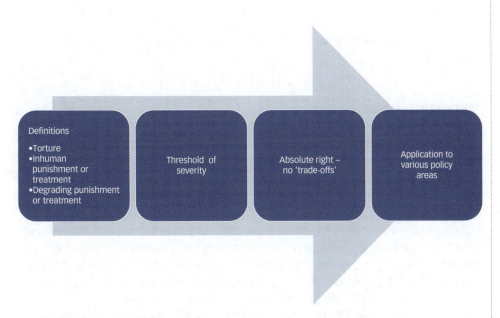

Figure 5.2 Outline of the main issues relating to Article 3

The duty to investigate: the procedural limb of Article 3

As with Article 2, a failure by the state to mount an official and effective investigation in the face of well-grounded allegations of torture or inhuman or degrading treatment can, in itself, be a breach of Article 3. In *El-Masri* (mentioned above) the failure by FYR Macedonia to investigate thoroughly the applicant's claims, despite the mounting body of evidence pointing to 'extraordinary' (illegal) 'rendition', breached Article 3. In *R (Am) v Secretary of State for the Home Department* [2009] EWCA Civ 219 the Home Secretary was alerted to possible breaches of Article 3 at an immigration detention centre but failed to hold an effective investigation. The Court of Appeal held that there was a breach, under the HRA, of the claimants' Article 3 rights.

As with Article 2, the investigation must be independent and able to get at the truth and identify who was responsible.

In cases where the claimant alleges breaches of Article 2 or 3 on the basis of serious ill-treatment by police or security services, it can be difficult to prove the facts. The ECtHR requires such serious allegations to be proved beyond a reasonable doubt by the claimant. However, where a person was last seen alive in the custody of the state or where they emerge from a police station battered and bruised, the Court may well determine that the burden of proof has now shifted to the state to prove there was not a breach of Article 2 or 3. The failure, properly and independently, to investigate may therefore mean that the state is held responsible for the substantive breach (not just the failure to investigate).

Deportation etc

Persons who are not British citizens can be 'removed' (if they are in the UK illegally) or 'deported' (as a consequence of a criminal conviction or because the Home Secretary thinks their presence is against the public interest); anyone can be 'extradited' if a foreign country wants to put them on trial. There is a clear body of jurisprudence (case law) from the ECtHR that to send someone to a country in which there is a real risk that they will be killed, tortured or treated inhumanely etc is itself a violation of Article 2 or Article 3 (e.g. *Chahal v United Kingdom* (1997) 23 EHRR 413). This is so no matter how great the threat the person may pose in the expelling country or how unpleasant their actions have been. The Court has steadfastly refused to budge on this point despite arguments by the UK and other countries that, in the case of persons posing a serious threat to national security (e.g. terrorist suspects), it ought to be able to balance the threat against the risk and deport if the threat to the expelling country is great and the risk of death or torture etc is low.

SUMMARY

Articles 2 and 3 impose a range of negative and positive duties on the state in order that the right to life is protected and people are not tortured or treated inhumanely. These duties can apply in a wide range of situations for which the state is responsible. These are important rights, indeed Article 3 is considered to be absolute. Both Articles 2 and 3 impose a duty on states to hold effective and independent investigations of alleged breaches.

ISSUES TO THINK ABOUT FURTHER

Article 2 and, especially, Article 3 represent the minimum standards of civilised behaviour states should abide by. Yet in recent years, in contexts such as the war against terrorism and the treatment of detainees by British forces overseas, they seem to have been disregarded. Ought these standards to be strengthened?

FURTHER READING

- Davis, H., *Human Rights Law Directions*, 2013, Oxford: OUP.
  This book provides a more detailed introduction to Articles 2 and 3; it refers to both Convention law and UK law under the HRA.
- Harris, D.J., O'Boyle, M. and Warbrick, C., *Law of the European Convention on Human Rights*, 2009, Oxford: OUP.
  Chapters 2 and 3 contain a comprehensive exploration of the Convention law.
- Greenberg, K.J., *The Torture Debate*, 2006, Cambridge: CUP.
  A series of essays, supported by documents, contributing to the issue of the use of torture by the US in the context of the 'war on terror'.

COMPANION WEBSITE

Additional content from the author is available on the companion website:
www.routledge.com/cw/beginningthelaw

Chapter 6
The right to liberty

LEARNING OBJECTIVES

On completing this chapter the reader should understand:

- The point of protecting liberty as a human right
- The scope of Article 5 ECHR and 'deprivation of liberty'
- The exclusive purposes for which a state can legitimately deprive a person of his or her liberty
- The importance of judicial supervision of the loss of liberty
- The additional rights under Article 5 ECHR relating to information and compensation.

INTRODUCTION: THE RIGHT TO LIBERTY

The right to liberty refers to personal, physical, liberty, to the right to decide for yourself where to live, where to go and who to visit, etc. Liberty in this sense is lost when someone else (a police officer, a prison officer, a kidnapper etc) takes you under his or her physical control and decides those things for you.

The recognition of the right to liberty

The need to protect a person's liberty in this sense is widely recognised in legal systems throughout the world. For example, English common law assumes that a person is free unless specific rules of law (usually Acts of Parliament) permit detention. Likewise, the Fifth Amendment to the US Constitution famously prevents the deprivation of liberty without 'due process of law'. The protection of liberty is widely found in international law such as Article 9 of the International Covenant on Civil and Political Rights.

Protect from arbitrary detention

It needs to be noted that the right is not about deprivation of liberty as such. Rather, it is the right not to be deprived of liberty arbitrarily. You should not be imprisoned just because those in power see it as politically convenient or for the public good. People should only lose their liberty following the application of clear rules of law, administered by an independent and impartial judiciary, and for a proper purpose. Any loss of liberty, other than on this basis, must be properly and quickly remedied.

A liberal and democratic society will recognise that there are proper purposes for which it is necessary to restrict an individual's liberty. Liberty may be outweighed by a legitimate need to punish or by the need to protect the public, specific individuals or to save the person concerned from self-harm. Obvious examples include the imprisonment of criminals convicted of serious crimes, the arrest of people suspected of offences and the detention for treatment or protection of those with serious mental health problems.

ARTICLE 5 ECHR THE RIGHT TO LIBERTY AND SECURITY

The European Convention on Human Rights deals with these issues on the basis of Article 5, which:

- asserts the general right to liberty and security,
- insists that any deprivation of liberty must be on the basis of law,
- describes the exclusive purposes for which states can detain people,
- requires there to be proper judicial supervision of the lawfulness of any loss of liberty, and
- requires (uniquely amongst Convention rights) compensation for those detained in violation of the right.

The text should be carefully read:

Article 5 Right to liberty and security

(1)   Everyone has the right to liberty and security of person. No one shall be deprived of his liberty save in the following cases and in accordance with a procedure prescribed by law:

(a)   the lawful detention of a person after conviction by a competent court;

(b)   the lawful arrest or detention of a person for non-compliance with the lawful order of a court or in order to secure the fulfilment of any obligation prescribed by law;

(c)   the lawful arrest or detention of a person effected for the purpose of bringing him before the competent legal authority on reasonable suspicion of having committed an offence or when it is reasonably considered necessary to prevent his committing an offence or fleeing after having done so;

(d)   the detention of a minor by lawful order for the purpose of educational supervision or his lawful detention for the purpose of bringing him before the competent legal authority;

(e)   the lawful detention of persons for the prevention of the spreading of infectious diseases, of persons of unsound mind, alcoholics or drug addicts or vagrants;

(f)   the lawful arrest or detention of a person to prevent his effecting unauthorised entry into the country or of a person against whom action is being taken with a view to deportation or extradition.

(2)   Everyone who is arrested shall be informed promptly, in a language which he understands, of the reasons for his arrest and of any charge against him.

(3)   Everyone arrested or detained in accordance with the provisions of paragraph 1(c) of this article shall be brought promptly before a judge or other officer authorised by law to exercise judicial power and shall be entitled to trial within a reasonable time or to release pending trial. Release may be conditioned by guarantees to appear for trial.

(4)   Everyone who is deprived of his liberty by arrest or detention shall be entitled to take proceedings by which the lawfulness of his detention shall be decided speedily by a court and his release ordered if the detention is not lawful.

(5)   Everyone who has been the victim of arrest or detention in contravention of the provisions of this article shall have an enforceable right to compensation.

Article 5(1)
- Has there been a deprivation of liberty?
- Consider the definition of 'deprivation of liberty' in European and UK case law.
- If the deprivation was not a direct state responsibility, is the state nevertheless under a positive duty to deal with it?

Article 5(1)
- Was the deprivation of liberty for one of the six purposes listed in article 5(1)(a)–(f)?
- Was the deprivation of liberty arbitrary?
- Was the deprivation of liberty consistent with the idea of 'law' (see Chapter 4 in this book).

Article 5(2)–(5)
- Was the person deprived of their liberty informed of the reason?
- Did the person deprived of their liberty have access to a 'court' capable of giving adequate remedies, including release, if the deprivation is unlawful (under Article 5(3) and (4)).
- Is there a duty to compensate?

Figure 6.1 Illustrates the issues that a court must consider when dealing with a claim under Article 5

The general right

The first thing to notice is that Article 5 starts with a general right to liberty and security. This means that there is a presumption in favour of liberty. Reasons for detaining persons must be sufficient to outweigh that presumption. The ECtHR not only requires the general criteria for detention to be satisfied but also that, in the particular circumstances, the patient's loss of liberty is 'necessary' (*Saadi v United Kingdom* (2008) 47 EHRR 17, para 70).

The general right can also mean that signatory states have a 'positive duty' (discussed in Chapter 4) to protect people from arbitrary loss of liberty at the hands of private parties or organisations whose authority may be wholly or mainly contractual. An example is *Storck v Germany* (2006) 43 EHRR 6 where an 18-year-old girl was detained in a private mental hospital at the request of her father and without her consent. The ECtHR held that the state had positive obligations under Article 5 which, in these circumstances, it had failed to fulfill (see paras 100–108).

Law and legality

The second sentence of Article 5 makes it clear that any 'deprivation of liberty' must be in accordance with a 'procedure prescribed by law'. Here we need to recall both the importance for human rights of the rule of law and the special 'autonomous' definition that the ECtHR has given to that term (see Chapter 4). Specifically, any interference with a person's liberty by the state has to be on a basis of law. This means not only must it be in conformity with national law (as recognised by national courts) but it must also meet the Convention standard for 'law'. Specifically the law must be:

- 'accessible' – the rule of law involved can be identified,
- 'foreseeable' – the rule of law involved is sufficiently clear, given the context, so that individuals can predict whether they are likely to be affected, and
- consistent with the values underlying the rule of law – the rule of law is linked to a general requirement that officials should not behave in an arbitrary way.

On-the-spot question

How is the concept of 'law' defined under the ECHR? Give at least one leading case in which this is found (check back to Chapter 4).

DEPRIVATION OF LIBERTY

Apart from the general duty, Article 5 only applies where there has been a 'deprivation of liberty'. The protections Article 5 guarantees do not, therefore, apply to someone who has merely been restricted in their movements or whose ordinary freedom to lead a normal life has been restricted. There is Article 2 of Protocol 4 of the Convention. This guarantees a person 'liberty of movement and the right to choose his residence'. However, the United Kingdom has not ratified the Protocol and it is not a 'Convention right' under the HRA; and, in any case, the right is highly qualified so that restrictions that are in the public interest are allowed.

'Deprivation of liberty' defined

Whether a person has been deprived of their liberty is a matter of fact measured against a legal test. In *Guzzardi v Italy* (1980) 3 EHRR 333, the ECtHR held that the difference between being deprived of liberty and being restricted in freedom of movement is a matter of degree. Crucially, deprivation of liberty included, but was not confined to, imprisonment. A person could be subject to a range of restrictions (none involving imprisonment) which, when taken together and considered in relation to the particular circumstances of the case, could amount to a deprivation of liberty.

The House of Lords followed this and other cases in decisions on control orders.

KEY CASE: *Secretary of State for the Home Department v JJ* **(2007) UKHL 45**

Background:

'Control orders' imposed various restrictions on the normal lives of terrorist suspects (these orders were replaced by T-PIMS – Terrorist Prevention and Investigation Measures, in 2012). Under the Prevention of Terrorism Act 2005, control orders were lawful so long as they did not deprive the controllee of his or her liberty.

JJ, the controllee, was required to stay in a small flat for 18 hours a day and was also subject to other restrictions.

The House of Lords held that there was a deprivation of liberty.

Principle established:

The flexible test in *Guzzardi* should be taken into account. Nevertheless, some of their Lordships put greater stress on the need for a core element of physical restraint. Lord Brown took the view that confinement of less than 14 to 16 hours could never be a deprivation of liberty. Other law lords took a less rigid approach which has been followed in later cases. However, if the element of confinement is for that period or less, other restrictive factors will have to be very stringent if the cumulative effect is a 'deprivation of liberty'.

The question of whether there has been a deprivation of liberty has come up in various contexts. For example:

- Care homes. There was a deprivation of liberty in respect of a vulnerable adult placed in a care home by a local authority who was not allowed to leave to be looked after by his wife (as he apparently wished). The crucial point was that, despite his considerable freedom within the home, he was not allowed to leave it (*JE v DE* (2006) EWHC 3459).
- Public order. In *Austin v Commissioner of Police of the Metropolis* [2009] UKHL 5 the House of Lords held that there would be no 'deprivation of liberty' if police, acting in good faith and proportionately, used 'kettling' techniques against demonstrators. These techniques involved hemming demonstrators in to a particular area for many hours. The requirement that police act proportionately is very important.

REASONS FOR DETENTION (ARTICLE 5(1))

In order to ensure that liberty is protected from arbitrary restrictions, Article 5 lays down the exclusive – the only – reasons for which states can deprive persons of their liberty. To detain someone for some other reason, even if done lawfully, with procedural fairness and with the public interest in mind, cannot be compatible with Article 5. Thus in *A v Secretary of State for the Home Department* [2004] UKHL 56, the government failed to persuade the House of Lords that detaining foreign suspects who were believed to be terrorists or with links to terrorism, was compatible with Article 5. Their detention could not be shown to be for one of the allowed reasons even though, in the government's view, it was in the public interest.

These reasons are listed in Article 5(1).

Punishment of convicted criminals

Article 5(1)(a) allows for the ordinary imprisonment of properly convicted criminals. So long as the criminal trial is lawful and fair the resulting imprisonment will be compatible with Article 5. Imprisonment must be 'lawful' and this includes the need for there to be a proportionate link between the offence and the punishment. However, Article 5 has not helped prisoners in the UK who are detained in prison longer than they otherwise might have been because of the refusal of the Home Secretary to fund rehabilitation courses. The Parole Board would only accept they were safe to release if they had attended these courses – *R (Wells) v Parole Board* [2009] UKHL 22.

Securing compliance with lawful orders and obligations

Article 5(1)(b) allows states to detain people in order to compel compliance with a lawful court order (e.g. a person refuses to take a blood test ordered by a court) or to ensure that an 'obligation prescribed by law' is fulfilled. This latter term is rather vauge and so the ECtHR requires it to be narrowly interpreted. The aim of detention must be to secure performance not to punish. In *R (Gillan) v Commissioner of Police for the Metropolis* [2006] UKHL 12, the House of Lords held that a police stop and search, if it went on long enough to involve a deprivation of liberty, could then be justified by reference to Article 5(1)(b) (the ECtHR in *Gillan v UK* (2010) 50 EHRR 45 did not comment on the point).

Arrest on reasonable suspicion of having committed a crime

Article 5(1)(c) authorises police and other state agencies to arrest and detain criminal suspects. The arrest must be:

- Lawful – in accordance with national laws which must be 'accessible', 'foreseeable' and non-arbitrary (i.e. they accord with the Convention idea of law, discussed in Chapter 4).
- Based on 'reasonable suspicion' – the national law need not require the arresting officers to have enough evidence on which to charge, but there must be 'some facts or information which would satisfy an objective observer that the person . . . may have committed the offence' (*O'Hara v UK* (2002) 34 EHRR 32, para 34); something more than a mere hunch. In *O'Hara* the applicant was arrested on suspicion based solely on evidence from anonymous informers. The ECtHR held that in the circumstances (terrorism) there was a sufficient evidential basis for reasonable suspicion.
- Proportionate – even if there is reasonable suspicion of an offence, the decision to arrest must still be proportionate (because proportionality is a general aspect of lawfulness). Under English law, the Police and Criminal Evidence Act 1984,

s 24, only allows an arrest if grounds exist and, furthermore, an arrest is 'necessary'.

- For an 'offence' – the arrested person must be suspected of behaviour that amounts to a criminal offence. In England a person can be detained to prevent a 'breach of the peace'. This, in itself, is not an offence. However it has been held to be close enough to criminal behaviour for such arrests not to violate Article 5 (*Steel v UK* (1999) 28 EHRR 603).
- In order to charge – the arrest must be 'for the purpose of bringing [the person] before the competent legal authority'. If the police detain people against whom they have reasonable suspicion, but the aim is, for example, to control a demonstration, if may not be compatible with Article 5.

Article 5(1)(c) allows a person to be detained in order to prevent the commission of offences. However, 'preventive detention' (detaining people merely because they are believed to be connected with crime) is inconsistent with the basic values of the rule of law. 'Internment' (e.g. imprisoning terrorist suspects) requires a 'derogation' from Article 5; and this means that the requirements of Article 15 must be satisfied (*Lawless v Ireland* (1979–80) 1 EHRR 15). This is discussed in Chapter 4.

Detention of minors

Article 5(1)(d) allows the detention of minors (under 18s) who are not being charged with criminal offences but might, for example, have serious behavioural difficulties. In such circumstances, minors can be detained so long as the place of detention can provide appropriate educational provision, although short term detention prior to transfer to such a place is permitted (*D.G. v Ireland* (2002) 35 EHRR 33). Article 5(1)(d) also allows minors to be detained who are, for example, going to be subject to a care order but who need to be detained immediately for their own protection. Nothing in Article 5(1)(d) prevents minors being detained for any of the other reasons in Article 5(1).

People with infectious diseases, the mentally ill, alcoholics and vagrants

Article 5(1)(e) allows states to have laws which permit the detention of the mentally ill etc. However there is a clear danger that laws could be drawn up and applied in ways that are unreasonable and oppress poor and vulnerable people. So the terms of Article 5(1)(e) need to be narrowly defined and any action taken under them needs to be proportionate and linked to behaviour (e.g. *Litwa v Poland* (2001) 33 EHRR 53, para 61). General laws which allow people to be detained, just because they are alcoholic or homeless etc are not be permitted.

Article 5(1)(e) has the most significance in respect of the mentally ill who sometimes ought to be placed, even against their will, in a mental hospital. This can be for assessment, treatment or protection.

KEY CASE: *Winterwerp v The Netherlands* (1979) 2 EHRR 387

Background:

W was compulsorily detained in a mental hospital. He was unable to have his position reviewed by a court.

Principle established:

The ECtHR laid down the basic criteria for detention of the mentally ill (see para 39). National laws and procedures should only permit a person to be deprived of their liberty when:

- the person is proved to be of 'unsound mind' (suffering a professionally recognised disorder, not merely that their behaviour is deviant);
- the mental disorder must be sufficiently serious in its effects to 'warrant' compulsory confinement in hospital (later cases have tightened this to a necessity test in the sense that the authorities should consider alternatives to detention);
- the validity of continuing detention requires the persistence of the mental disorder.

Deportation

Article 5(1)(f) allows people to be detained with a view to their being lawfully deported or removed from the country. Detention is only allowed if deportation or removal is being diligently pursued. In the famous 'Belmarsh' case (*A v Secretary of State for the Home Department* (2004) UKHL 56) foreign terrorist suspects could not be deported because of the risk of torture in the receiving country. As a result they were imprisoned without trial. In the circumstances it could not be said that deportation was being diligently pursued and so detention was not compatible with Article 5(1)(e).

A controversial point is that detention, for this reason, does not need to be strictly necessary and can be done for reasons of administrative convenience; nor is it necessary for the state to prove that the detainee would be otherwise likely to try and escape and avoid deportation – the UK's position was upheld by the ECtHR in *Saadi v United Kingdom* (2008) 47 EHRR 17. It is still the case, though, that detention must not be arbitrary. Thus it is unlawful (and in breach of Article 5) for the authorities to detain a deportee without regard to their published policies on detention (*R (WL) v SSHD* [2011] UKSC 12).

INFORMATION (ARTICLE 5(2))

Article 5(1)(a)–(e) is concerned with the permissible reasons for detention. Article 5(2)–(5) stipulates basic rights that anyone deprived of their liberty for a proper reason is entitled to.

Under Article 5(2) a person deprived of their liberty must be informed of the reason. The point is to ensure:

- that people understand why they are losing their liberty; but also
- that a detained person is able to mount an informed and appropriate legal challenge in the courts.

English law on arrest (s 28, Police and Criminal Evidence Act 1984) has a clear provision requiring police to give a non-technical reason for the loss of liberty.

JUDICIAL SUPERVISION (ARTICLE 5(3) AND 5(4))

At the heart of the right to liberty is that any deprivation of liberty must be properly authorised by the law. Judges (such as magistrates or tribunal members) have the primary responsibility to ensure that any arrest, imprisonment or other detention has a proper legal basis. The applicable national laws must be 'accessible', 'foreseeable' and compatible with the underlying values of the rule of law (see Chapter 4). This applies not only to the initial detention but also to the full term for which a person is detained. At all times the loss of liberty must be properly authorised by law and, if the legal basis on which a person has been detained no longer applies, there need to be legal procedures by which their release can be ordered. Under English law, for example, the High Court can issue the writ of habeas corpus to order the release of a person unlawfully detained. These days it has less practical importance than other specifically tailored remedies and procedures: such as application to the Parole Board, for life sentence prisoners, and to mental health tribunals for detained patients. The procedures and remedies provided by the bodies need to be adequate in the circumstances to meet the requirements of Article 5(3) and 5(4).

Article 5(3)

Article 5(3) refers to those arrested, usually by the police, on reasonable suspicion of having committed a criminal offence (i.e. deprivations of liberty which must be compatible with Article 5(1)(c)). In *McKay v UK* (2007) 44 EHRR 41, a Grand Chamber understood Article 5(3) to be referring to two distinct issues.

Review at the time of arrest

A detainee is entitled to a prompt review by a judge or magistrate of the lawfulness of his or her arrest. This review can deal with issues such as whether there were reasonable grounds for the suspicion and whether the arrest was otherwise lawful (compatible with national laws which also meet the Convention standard of lawfulness). There are three central requirements:

- Promptness. The ECtHR has not laid down specific time periods but in *Brogan v UK* (1989) 11 EHRR 117 detention for four days as an anti-terrorist measure, at the behest of the executive and without access to a court, was too much. In England, under the Police and Criminal Evidence Act 1984, 'ordinary' criminal suspects must be brought before a magistrate within 24 hours after being charged and, at the most, after 36 hours of pre-charge detention by the police. Terrorist suspects can be detained under the Terrorism Act 2000 (as amended) for up to 14 days, but any detention beyond an initial 48 hours must be authorised by a District Judge.
- State responsibility. It is the state's duty to ensure that law and practice requires this prompt review. It must not be left to the detainee's initiative.
- Judicial power. The lawfulness of the initial detention must be tested before a proper judicial authority. This means, in particular, that the judge, magistrate or other judicial officer must be independent, particularly of the police and prosecuting authority. They must also have sufficient authority to be able to order the release of someone unlawfully detained (e.g. because of the absence of reasonable suspicion). Finally, the judicial process must be fair in the sense, for example, that there is an 'adversarial' hearing based on 'equality of arms'. This means that the detainee is able to know of and challenge the reasons for arrest and do so in a hearing in which he or she is treated on an equal basis with the police and prosecution.

Bail or release

The second issue under Article 5(3) relates to the period between being charged and coming to trial – this can be many months.

There is a presumption in favour of bail – the release of the suspect during this period. National laws can allow 'remand' (imprisonment during this period) if there are 'relevant and sufficient reasons' to refuse bail. These include a significant risk that the defendant will:

- abscond,
- pervert the course of justice, or
- commit further offences.

The seriousness of the offence should not be a relevant issue. The risk of public disorder, resulting from the release of an unpopular defendant, can be. Automatic refusal of bail for certain offences or types of offenders is likely to be incompatible with Article 5(3).

Where bail is refused and the defendant remanded in custody, Article 5(3) requires trial within a 'reasonable time'. The ECtHR refuses to lay down time periods *'in abstracto'* – generally, independently of the facts of a particular case. However it does require the authorities, in the circumstances, to be actively preparing the trial and not allowing the defendant to languish in jail (see, for example, *Erdem v Germany* (2002) 35 EHRR 15).

Article 5(3) links with Article 6, which requires a trial within a 'reasonable time'.

Article 5(4)

Judicial supervision of the lawfulness of any detention, under any of the grounds in Article 5(1), is required by Article 5(4). This is the habeas corpus principle by which national laws and procedures must provide a right of access to a court so that anyone can challenge the lawfulness of their detention.

Access to a court

So far as ordinary convicted prisoners are concerned, the fact that they had a fair trial and rights to appeal satisfies Article 5(4).

Serious or repeat offenders can be held for an 'indeterminate sentence' (e.g. the mandatory life sentence for murder). Prisoners are held for a fixed period after which they may be released on licence but only if it is considered safe to do so. Article 5(4) means that the decision on release must be taken by a judicial body and not the executive (who may be influenced by improper political considerations). In England and Wales, the Parole Board performs this function and must meet the requirements of Article 5(4).

Detained mental health patients have, in England and Wales, regular and continuing access to mental health tribunals.

Other detainees may challenge their detention in the High Court (usually by judicial review) though they may also be able to achieve the same effect by challenging the reason for their detention, as where a detained deportee challenges the decision to deport before an immigration and asylum tribunal.

Fair procedure

The reviewing body need not be a 'court' but it must be judicial in the sense of being properly independent and operating on the basis of a procedure which, like under Article 5(3) above, is adversarial and based on the equality of arms between the executive and the detained person. Most importantly it must be able to require, not just recommend, the release of the detained person if the grounds of lawful detention no longer exist.

KEY CASE: *H.L. v UK* (2005) 40 EHRR 32

Background:

H.L. was held in a mental health institution. He had been detained 'informally' and not under the Mental Health Act 1983, and therefore he did not have access to a mental health tribunal. The ECtHR held there was a breach of Article 5(4).

Principle established:

Remedies must not just exist they must also be effective. The remedies available to H.L. were: 'judicial review' of the decision to detain him, seeking a writ of habeas corpus or bringing a civil action for negligence or false imprisonment. In the context none of these remedies could guranteee H.L.'s Article 5 rights.

On-the-spot question

 Article 5(3) and (4) requires that a court or similar body assessing the lawfulness of a deprivation of liberty must act on the basis of a fair procedure. What is meant by that?

COMPENSATION

The importance of the right to liberty is demonstrated by the right, under Article 5(5), to compensation. This must be paid to a person who has been detained in ways that are incompatible with the rest of Article 5. Detention in breach of Article 5 is not necessarily the same thing as a wrong conviction. Wrongful conviction can happen in respect of entirely fair trials.

This is the only express reference to compensation in the Convention, although other rights can be remedied through the principle of 'just satisfaction'.

SUMMARY

Article 5 guarantees the right not to be arbitrarily deprived of physical liberty. At its heart are two principal ideas: liberty should only be lost for purposes generally accepted as being reasonable, and loss of liberty needs to be strictly controlled by the law and the courts.

ISSUES TO THINK ABOUT FURTHER

Are there circumstances in which the authorities ought to have the power to detain a person because he or she is believed to be a serious threat to the life and freedom of others? If so, could this power be compatible with Article 5?

FURTHER READING

- Harris, O'Boyle, Bates and Buckley, *Law of the European Convention on Human Rights,* 2nd edn, 2009, Oxford: OUP, Chapter 5.
  A comprehensive survey of the law on Article 5.
- Fenwick, H., 'Marginalising human rights: breach of the peace, "kettling", the Human Rights Act and public protest' (2009) *Public Law*, October, 737–65.
  A discussion of Article 5 in the context of public order.
- Ewing, K. and Than, J., 'The continuing futility of the Human Rights Act' (2008) *Public Law*, Winter, 668–93.
  This critical article contains an interesting section on the applicability of Article 5 in the counter-terrorism context.

COMPANION WEBSITE

Additional content from the author is available on the companion website:
www.routledge.com/cw/beginningthelaw

Chapter 7
The right to a fair hearing

LEARNING OBJECTIVES

On completing this chapter the reader should understand:

- The main terms of Article 6, the Convention right protecting the right to a fair trial (but also that there are other rights to a fair hearing such as in Article 5(3) and (4) – see Chapter 6)
- The kinds of trial or hearing which are covered by Article 6 and the kinds which are not covered
- Some of the principal rights that are inherent in the concept of a 'fair . . . hearing' – Article 6(1)
- The application of Article 6 specifically to criminal charges in Article 6(2) (presumption of innocence) and Article 6(3) (defendants' rights)
- The extent to which Article 6 rights are flexible and context-dependent.

INTRODUCTION

The right to a fair trial deals with procedures and can sound dull. It is not. Rights without remedies are pointless and it is through court hearings that remedies can be ordered. Defendants in criminal charges are up against the full might of the state. Litigants in civil proceedings may be taking on massive corporations who execise great economic power. It is vital that these trials and other procedures are fair and that even the weakest or most unpleasant persons are treated equally and are able to make their cases or defend themselves under equal terms with the powerful. This is central to the rule of law and it is what distinguishes the administraton of justice in a decent society from the show trials of dictatorships.

A right to a fair trial is, therefore, widely recognised. It is implied by Magna Carta (1215). It is an important feature of written constitutions (such as the US Constitution, 1789, which requires 'due process' of law). Likewise it is an important principle of international law, expressed in the UN Declaration of Human Rights (Articles 10 and 11) and given fuller legal effect by the International Covenant on Civil and Political Rights (Article 14).

UK LAW: ARTICLE 6, THE HRA AND THE COMMON LAW

In the European Convention on Human Rights, Article 6 gurantees the 'right to a fair trial' to claimants in civil cases and to defendants in criminal trials. Article 6 rights are, of course, given effect in UK law through the terms of the Human Rights Act 1998 (HRA). Procedures before the courts and tribunals of the UK tend to be found in:

- primary legislation (such as the Senior Courts Act 1981, the Police and Criminal Evidence Act 1984) or the Tribunals Courts and Enforcement Act 2007,
- secondary legislation (such as the Civil Procedure Rules or the **tribunal rules**).

Section 3 HRA requires this primary and secondary legislation to be interpreted consistently with Article 6 (unless it is really impossible). Likewise, the courts and tribunals are expressly defined as 'public authorities' and so, under s 6 HRA, must act compatibly with Convention rights.

Key Definition

Courts and tribunals: In England the 'Senior courts' are the High Court, the Crown Court and the Court of Appeal (all subordinate to the Supreme Court of the UK).

Other courts, such as the County Court and Magistrates Court, are established by Acts of Parliament which define the 'jurisdiction' of these courts – the types of cases they can lawfully decide.

'Tribunals' are court-like bodies which are established by statute to decide particular issues often dealing with disputes between an individual and a government department. In England many tribunals are part of the 'First Tier Tribunal' with an appeal to the 'Upper Tribunal'.

Article 6

Article 6 guarantees a general right to a fair hearing etc with additional rights for criminal defendants. It should be noted that fair hearing rights are also found expressly in other places. Article 5(4) gives a person deprived of his or her liberty a right to go to court to have the legality of their detention tested by a judge. The procedure must be fair. Other rights can also be violated by the failure of the state to provide a fair procedure in the context. For example: long delays in dealing with property disputes can violate Article 1 of the First Protocol (the right to the 'protection of property') – *Sporrong and Lönnroth v Sweden* (1983) 5 EHRR 35.

The common law

Despite Article 6 and other Convention rights, it is wrong not to understand the long-standing impact of common law on fair procedures in England and Wales. Judges are given considerable discretion on the way in which they conduct trials and deal with issues such as the admissibility of evidence. The common law rules of 'natural justice' give people an actionable right to a fair and impartial hearing. They apply widely, but in particular to magistrates, tribunals and also administrative bodies (like council licencing committees) taking decisions which directly affect an individuals rights or their 'legitimate expectations' of a government body.

The focus of this chapter is on Article 6.There are two principal issues:

- to what trials and hearings does Article 6 apply; and
- what is the content of Article 6 rights?

APPLICATION OF ARTICLE 6

Consider the trial or hearing in issue
- Does the hearing involve a persons civil rights and obligations?
OR
- Does it involve a criminal charge?

If yes to either
- Is the hearing 'determining' these civil rights and obligations of criminal charge or is it more preliminary?

If yes
- Article 6(1) applies to trials determining civil rights and obligations.
- Article 6(1) and (2) and (3) apply to trials determining criminal charges.

Figure 7.1 Summary of the issues about the application of Article 6

A person can rely on his or her Article 6 only when a court or tribunal etc is 'determining' 'civil rights and obligations' or a 'criminal trial'.

The distinction made in the Article between civil or criminal trials matters. If the trial or hearing is determining a person's 'civil rights and obligations' then there is just the general right to 'a fair and public hearing within a reasonable time by an independent and impartial tribunal established by law' (Article 6(1)). Where a 'criminal charge' is being determined, however, the accused person has not only this general right but also additional protection under Article 6(2) and (3) such as the right to be presumed innocent and other rights necessary for an effective defence.

Civil rights and obligations

'Civil rights and obligations' include private law rights such as those derived from contract, property (including intellectual property) or the law of torts. But the term is more extensive and has been applied, for example, to hearings determining whether a person has a right to pursue a profession or whether (most) Convention rights have been violated.

Criminal law

Criminal law has an autonomous meaning under the Convention. This means that whether a matter is criminal or civil is measured by the Convention standard and is not just dependent on how a matter is described under domestic law. In essence, a criminal procedure is one whose main point is to decide whether a person should be punished.

KEY CASE: *Ezeh v UK* (2004) 39 EHRR 1

Background:

E, a prisoner, was accused of threatening to kill his probation officer. He was charged with a prison disciplinary offence though he could have been charged with a criminal offence. He requested representation at the hearing before the prison governor and was refused.

First he argued that representation was necessary under common law 'natural justice'; this was refused.

Then he argued he had a right to legal representation under Article 6(3)(c). However this provision would only apply if the prison governor was determining a 'criminal charge'.

Principle established:

The European Court of Human Rights (ECtHR) held that though the offence with which E was charged was classed, under English law, as a disciplinary offence, at its heart this was a criminal matter. If the governor found E guilty he could impose 'additional days' in prison as a punishment.

Therefore the governor was determining a criminal charge and Article 6(3)(c) should have been applied.

Criminal or civil?

All this matters because, in various contexts, such as anti-social behaviour, mental health, child protection and anti-terrorism, Parliament has introduced protective measures. These may significantly interfere with a person's freedom of action. Often they can be obtained from a court on the basis of **hearsay** evidence or evidence which is not fully disclosed to the parties.

Key Definition

Hearsay: The evidence is of a person who is not present in court and who cannot be cross-examined.

If such measures are considered to be 'criminal' then the specific rights in Articles 6(2) and (3) apply and these include a specific right to examine witnesses (Article 6(3)(d)). In respect of determinations of civil rights, however, such rights are just inferences from the general right to a fair hearing and, consequently, they are more context-dependant and flexible. The matter is, however, complex. In *R (McCann) v Crown Court at Manchester* [2002] UKHL 39 the House of Lords held that a magistrate imposing an 'Asbo' (Anti-Social Behaviour Order) was determining a civil, not a criminal, matter. However, the impact of an Asbo was so severe that the magistrate should be satisfied beyond a reasonable doubt that the Asbo was necessary – i.e. to the criminal standard of proof.

Public law

There is a middle range of hearings that, in the Convention sense, are neither civil nor criminal. Matters which are strictly public law and do not also involve private rights, are outside the scope of Article 6. Hearings dealing with tax and immigration have been held, by the ECtHR, not to involve private rights but, rather, civic duties or privileges which are within the discretion of the state. As such they are not covered by Article 6 at all. Difficult questions arise over hearings determining disputes about welfare (pensions, unemployment pay, housing entitlement etc). The extent to which Article 6 applies depends on the degree to which courts, tribunals and officials are giving effect to settled rights in contrast to them exercising discretion within a policy framework. Where the issue is clearly the latter, Article 6 may not apply. It needs to be remembered, though, that 'public law' decisions of this kind can still be challenged, in England and Wales, through an application for judicial review and one of the grounds of such an application is that the procedure is unfair – lacking 'natural justice'.

Determination

Article 6 only applies when a civil right or criminal charge is being 'determined' by the court, tribunal etc whose procedure is being questioned. Usually, therefore, Article 6 does not apply to preliminary matters – such as the procedures for investigating a complaint against an individual prior to deciding whether to take further action. Whether a matter is merely preliminary can be difficult to define. The UK case, *G v Governors of X School*, illustrates some of the issues.

KEY CASE: *R (G) v Governors of X School* [2011] UKSC 30

Background:

Sexual misbehaviour was alleged against G, a classroom assistant at X School. G was sacked by the governors on the basis of an investigation and hearing at which he was denied representation. If Article 6(1) applied, representation in these circumstances would be required.

Consequently, the school had a statutory duty to report G to the Independent Safeguarding Authority (ISA). The ISA had the power to deny G the right to continue working as a teacher.

Principle established:

The UKSC held that right to practice a profession is a civil right (see, for example, *Le Compte v Belgium* (1983) 5 EHRR 533).

Normally, however, the procedure by which an employer dismisses an employee will not be determining this right: this is done by the County Court or Employment Tribunal to whom the employee can apply to test the legality of the dismissal. Court or Tribunal procedures must satisfy Article 6.

It was the ISA which determined G's civil right. If the dismissal by the school was a significant factor in the decision by the ISA, Article 6 rights would apply to the school as well as the ISA – the law would see it as a single procedure. However, on the facts the ISA made its own assessment and did not rely on the school's view.

Therefore Article 6 rights did not apply to the dismissal proceedings.

On-the-spot question

What kinds of hearings or trials are NOT covered by Article 6?

SUBSTANCE OF A FAIR HEARING: CIVIL AND CRIMINAL HEARINGS

Having considered the kinds of hearing to which Article 6 applies, we should now discuss the content of those rights.

'Fair hearing' – inherent rights

Civil litigants and criminal defendants enjoy a right to a fair hearing. However, Article 6 says little about what that means in practice. So the substance and application of the right is left to the way Article 6 is interpreted by the ECtHR and domestic courts under the HRA.

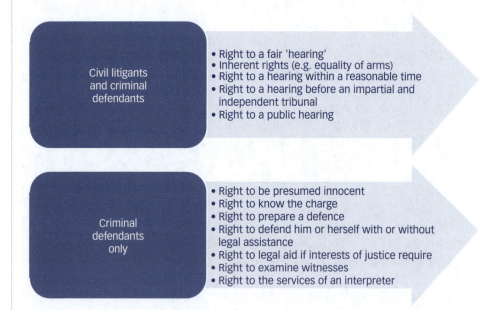

Figure 7.2 Summary of the rights of civil litigants and criminal defendants

European countries have very different legal systems and approaches to fairness. In particular there are significant differences between the common law approach of England and Wales and the 'civilian' system found on the continent. The role of ECtHR is not to enforce any particular system. It does not, for example, require a jury. Its concern is with the overall fairness of the procedure used, whatever it is.

What the ECtHR has done is to identify a number of basic rights that are inherent in, or implied by, the idea of a fair hearing. These are rights without which it would be hard to see a procedure as fair. Two of these inherent rights are of great importance:

- The right of 'access to court'. There may be a breach of Article 6 if some legal rule or administrative practice has the effect of preventing a person from pursuing a legal right through the courts. A breach of this right is arguable if, for example, the law allows the prison authorities to restrict a prisoner's ability to contact a solicitor and pursue a case against the prison authorities, or if court fees are raised so high that they deter the would-be litigant.
- The principle of 'equality of arms'. Under this principle a hearing is only fair if all parties have equal access to the evidence. Systems which, for example, allow the prosecution to have special access to the judge, not enjoyed by the defence, may breach this principle. In the counter-terrorism context in the UK, there are various procedures which arguably undermine the principle. An example is that a person can be deported without knowing the details of the evidence against him or her.

Inherent rights are not treated as absolute. They are flexible and the specifics of what they require depend very much on context and circumstance. However, there are limits to this flexibility. The courts must ensure that the 'essence' of the right is maintained. Any restrictions must be for a legitimate purpose and proportionate and there should be counter-balancing measures to protect the person involved. Restrictions which deny the protection of Article 6 altogether will be violations.

KEY CASE: *A v UK* (2009) 49 EHRR 29

Background:

AF and others were foreign terrorist suspects held in prison without trial after '9/11'. Allthough they could challenge their position before a special tribunal (the Special Immigration Appeals Commission) they were not allowed to see the 'closed evidence' upon which the Commission relied. AF alleged a breach of the fair hearing provision in Article 5 (the right to liberty, see Chapter 6) – but the position adopted by the ECtHR applies to Article 6 as well.

Principle established:

A Grand Chamber held that equality of arms had been violated. If, as in this case, the 'sole or decisive' evidence against a person was unknown to them and could not be challenged, the right to a fair hearing was violated. The existence of counter-balancing provisions (such as the use of **special counsel**) could not remedy this. The very essence of the right was lost.

This point is discussed further below in respect of Article 6(3).

Key Definition

Special counsel: These are security-cleared advocates, who can see all the secret ('closed') material but cannot disclose it to or discuss it with their clients.

Overall, the ECtHR requires an 'adversarial' approach in the limited sense that a litigant or criminal defendant must be able to make his or her case in an effective way. The principles of access to court and equality of arms embody this principle. So do other issues such as whether or not, in the context, an oral hearing is necessary for fairness, where the burden of proof lies, the ability of a litigant or defendant (such as a child) to follow proceedings and whether, in the circumstances, representation is necessary. As said above, it is not for the ECtHR to lay down particular rules and practices but to decide whether, in the circumstances, the procedure was fair.

Delay in proceedings is a matter, expressly mentioned in Article 6, which can affect the overall fairness of civil or criminal proceedings. The ECtHR does not identify particular time periods (e.g. the maximum time a prisoner can be kept on remand before trial) but is concerned with what is acceptable in the circumstances.

Independence and impartiality

A court or tribunal subject to Article 6 must be independent and impartial.

Broadly speaking:

- Independence – courts and tribunals determining civil rights and obligations or criminal charges must make their own decision and not allow themselves to be persuaded by the views of others, especially those of the government.
- Impartiality – such bodies must not be swayed by prior assumptions or prejudices which might create a possibility that the decision would be arrived at unfairly.

There is nothing new in this under domestic law. English common law already gives a remedy if courts, tribunals and administrative bodies allow their freedom to decide cases to be 'fettered' by outside bodies or if they allow themselves to be dictated to by others, including political superiors. Likewise, they must be seen to be acting without 'bias'. These rules of 'natural justice' were amended a little to bring them in line with Article 6.

Article 6 has had a significant impact in the UK in respect of independence. Some important and long-standing institutions and procedures have been scrutinised under Article 6 and, because they lacked independence, needed to be changed. Thus the system of courts martial had to be reformed because the links between the officer who ordered the court martial and the court were too close, setting up a possible presumption of guilt (*Findlay v UK* (1997) 24 EHRR 221); and employment tribunal rules had to be changed in respect of cases in which the Secretary of State, who appointed the members, was a party (*Scanfuture v Secretary of State for Trade and Industry* [2001] ICR 1096). In Scotland radical reform of the system of appointing temporary sheriffs (magistrates) was required following *Starrs v Ruxton* (2000) SLT 42.

Some decisions taken by administrative bodies (such as local authority planning committees or housing departments) can involve determining civil rights. If so, any internal system of review or appeal is likely to lack the independence required by Article 6. If such bodies had to organise themselves so as to satisfy Article 6 there would be huge consequences for efficient public administration (e.g. if all housing decisions had to be tested by a specially constituted independent judicial body). The way out of this dilemma is that Article 6 is satisfied so long as there is a right of appeal to a court, such as the County Court. So long as this appellate court or tribunal has 'full jurisdiction', in the sense of being able to deal with all the relevant issues of fact and law, Article 6 can be satisfied.

Openness

The other basic right is to a public hearing and to the decision being given in public.

It is a long-standing principle, found in common law as much as in Article 6, that justice must be done in public. There is both an individual right to a trial in public but also a strong public interest in open justice. As always, though, there are exceptions. Article 6 allows the exclusion of the media and the public from trials when this is necessary, for example, to protect the rights of juveniles or other vulnerable persons. But exceptions need to be carefully scrutinised. There is an increasing tendency in the UK to have secret proceedings in the context of trials and hearings dealing with national security and anti-terrorism. Article 6 can allow this subject to proper scrutiny. The danger is that such proceedings can be used to keep wrong doing, particularly complicity in torture, from the public eye. This matter is discussed further, below, in the context of the withholding of evidence.

On-the-spot question

 Consider the disciplinary procedures at the place where you study or work – how fair are they?

SUBSTANCE OF A FAIR HEARING: CRIMINAL CHARGES

Persons being tried for a criminal offence enjoy not only the full gamut of rights under Article 6(1) (interpreted in the context of a criminal offence) but also additional rights which are those which aim to protect the defence in a criminal process. Again, these rights are also found in common law and statute. Although there is much common ground, there are, as will be demonstrated, a number of issues where Article 6 may have made a difference.

Article 6(2) – the right to be presumed innocent

There are few, if any, principles of criminal law more fundamental than the right of the defendant to be presumed innocent and the consequential duty is on the prosecuting authorities to prove the case 'beyond a reasonable doubt'. This right is firmly entrenched in the common law and is reinforced by Article 6. It is inherent in both the general idea of a fair trial (Article 6(1)) and in Article 6(2).

The extent to which this principle requires a defendant to have the right to remain silent and the right not to be tried on the basis of evidence he or she has been compelled to produce, has been problematic.

English law, for instance, allows a jury to infer guilt from the silence of a defendant in certain circumstances. Embodying the general approach of the ECtHR, these provisions will not violate Article 6 so long as there is some supporting evidence upon which the conviction can be based and thus the essence of the right is not destroyed (see *Murray v UK* (1996) 22 EHRR 29).

KEY CASE: *O'Halloran v UK* (2008) 46 EHRR 21

Background:

Owners of cars caught on speed cameras receive a letter asking whether they were driving the car. It is a criminal offence not to answer truthfully. That answer can then be used as evidence in a separate prosecution, of the owner, for speeding.

O'H argued that he was being convicted, for speeding, on the basis of evidence he had been compelled to provide and this destroyed his right to be presumed innocent of the speeding charge.

Principle established:

The right to silence was not absolute. In the circumstances, particularly road safety and the fact that driving was a licenced and regulated activity, the interference with the right was proportionate. The court dealt with the right to silence as inherent in a 'fair hearing' in Article 6(1); Article 6(2) raised no separate points.

Another commonly found feature of English criminal law is the 'reverse onus' defence. This is where, if a certain set of facts are proved, the defendant is presumed guilty unless he or she can prove otherwise. For example, the occupier of premises on which explosives are found is presumed to be guilty of an offence unless he or she can prove that they had no knowledge of the explosives. Article 6 can be used to ensure that the burden of proof remains with the prosecution. Normally the defendant's explanation for what happened will be accepted unless the prosecution can prove that it is false or inadequate (e.g. *Sheldrake v DPP* [2004] UKHL 43). Again, this is a matter that engages both Article 6(2) and the general right to fairness in Article 6(1).

Article 6(3)(a)–(e)

Criminal defendants enjoy the general right to a fair hearing in Article 6(1) and the specific rights inherent in it and also the presumption of innocence in Article 6(2). In addition, Article 6(3) provides a criminal defendant with a number of basic rights concerning the fair conduct of the trial. Thus a defendant must:

- know the case against him or her;
- have adequate time and facilities to prepare a defence;
- be able to defend him or herself; and this includes a right to be represented and have the benefit of legal aid if 'the interests of justice so require';
- to cross examine prosecution witnesses and have equal rights as the prosecution to compel the attendance of and examine defence witnesses;
- to use an interpreter if necessary.

These rights are also strongly guarded principles of fairness in the common law. Nevertheless, the fact that they are express rights in the Convention may give them a stronger presence and make them less vulnerable to being weakened by statutory change. The issue of tension between the common law approach and the Convention showed itself in *Horncastle*.

KEY CASE: *R v Horncastle* [2009] UKSC 14

Background:

In *Al-Khawaja v UK* (2009) 49 EHRR 1, a chamber of the ECtHR had held that a conviction based 'solely or to a decisive extent' on hearsay evidence would necessarily violate Article 6.

In English law, an Act of Parliament gave judges discretion to admit **hearsay** in a criminal trial. H and C were convicted on evidence given in court from witnesses who had died or absconded. This was decisive evidence on which H and C were convicted.

> Principle established:
>
> The UKSC declined to follow *Al-Khawaja*. A conviction solely or decisively based on hearsay could, nevertheless, be fair overall because of protections in the Act of Parliament and because of the discretion of judges to exclude evidence if it would be unfair to admit it (see s 78 Police and Criminal Evidence Act 1984).
>
> In *Al-Khawaja v UK* (2012) 54 EHRR 23, a Grand Chamber of the ECtHR departed somewhat from the chamber and held that the sole or decisive rule was not an absolute. Later cases in the UK have allowed decisive hearsay evidence if tests of reliability and other protections are satisfied (e.g. *R v Riat* [2012] EWCA Crim 1509).

The underlying human rights issue in *Horncastle* is the extent to which a criminal defendant has an absolute right, under Article 6(3)(d), to know the case against him or herself and be able to challenge and test the evidence in court. The same issue has given rise to great political and legal controversy in the context of counter-terrorism law. Here the context is 'civil', engaging Article 6(1), rather than criminal trials. Special powers, such as public interest deportations or the imposition of controls (Terrorist Prevention and Investigation Measures) on suspects, all involve hearings before judges. The evidence may have been obtained from a foreign power under the condition that it would not be disclosed. On the other hand the evidence may be unreliable or suggest that there has been torture or other ill-treatment which the applicant needs to have disclosed if he is to defend him or herself or pursue a legal action. The UK's answer has been to use **special counsel**. Under the Justice and Security Act 2013 use of special counsel in closed hearings will be permitted for civil actions (such as suing UK officials in Tort for alleged complicity in torture).

SUMMARY

Article 6 guarantees rights to a fair hearing for those pursuing their private rights ('civil rights') in the courts and those who have been accused of crimes. As some of the cases discussed above illustrate, Article 6 rights are involved in some of the great legal controversies of the times, such as over counter-terrorism and anti-social behaviour. Article 6 is an important inhibition on governments, acting in good faith, for the public interest, who are trying to push back the boundaries of the rule of law. Though Article 6 is clearly flexible and what it requires can the affected by context, the courts must, nevertheless, uphold the essence of a fair trial.

ISSUES TO THINK ABOUT FURTHER

Maintaining fair trials in the national security context remains controversial. The Justice and Security Act 2013 alows the wider use of closed evidence in civil actions against the government. Critics argue that this may mean that evidence of government complicity in torture might not be publicly disclosed and that the rule of law, generally, will be weakened. The government's defence is that this allows the evidence to be tested under judicial standards and officials to defend themselves from extremely serious allegations.

FURTHER READING

- Fordham, M., 'Security and Fair Trials: the UK Constitution in Transition' (2012) *Judicial Review*, 17(3), 187–202.
  A thorough examination of the law on closed material procedures in the context of the Justice and Security Bill (now enacted).
- *Begum v Tower Hamlets LBC* [2003] UKHL 5, paras 25–35.
  In these paragraphs Lord Hoffmann explains 'civil rights and obligations' in the context of administrative decisions.
- Clayton, R. and Tomlinson, H., *Fair Trial Rights*, 2010, Oxford: OUP.
  A full exploration of both common law and Convention law on the issue.

COMPANION WEBSITE

Additional content from the author is available on the companion website:
www.routledge.com/cw/beginningthelaw

Chapter 8
Rights to privacy and property

LEARNING OBJECTIVES

On completing this chapter the reader should understand:

- The impact of Article 8 in providing a legal basis for challenges to interferences with private and family life, home and correspondence
- The structure of Article 8 as a 'qualified right'
- The protection of the right to peaceful enjoyment of possessions guaranteed by Article 1 of the First Protocol
- The context of both of these Convention rights in respect of broader ideas about privacy and property.

INTRODUCTION

Being a 'person', a full human being, implies that there should be areas of life that remain under that person's sole control and subject solely to his or her choices. There should be areas of life that are not to be controlled or interfered with by others – such as police or civil servants acting under the general law or an employer acting on the basis of a contract of employment. This is, perhaps, the basic idea of 'privacy'. The European Court of Human Rights (ECtHR) sometimes refers to 'an "inner circle" in which the individual may live his own personal life as he chooses' (*Niemietz v Germany* (1993) 16 EHRR 97). As we shall see, however, the various rights grouped together in Article 8 (respect for private and family life, home and correspondence) include, but go well beyond, this limited idea of privacy. It moves in the direction of being a right to live your life as you please subject to the reasonable restraints of others – where, obviously, attention is then focused on the nature of those reasonable restraints and who decides their impact.

ENGLISH LAW

The common law of England and Wales has not developed a legally enforceable concept of privacy in itself. However, important aspects of private life are protected by law in a variety of ways. For example:

- criminal law protects bodily integrity by deterring physical attacks; it protects rights to property by deterring burglary etc;

- property law gives 'owners' rights over land, goods, inventions etc which can be enforced against others;
- the tort of defamation protects reputation;
- confidential information can be maintained by injunctions from the courts;
- administrative law can remedy unlawful invasion of privacy by officials.

These provisions of English domestic law are found in Acts of Parliament and court rulings. The Human Rights Act 1998 (HRA) requires that they be interpreted and applied in ways that are consistent with Convention rights (unless this is prevented by clear statutory words). The two main Convention rights that relate to a person's privacy are Article 8 and Article 1 of the First Protocol.

The common law does not provide a remedy for a breach of privacy that cannot be brought within the definition of one of the crimes, torts or laws of property referred to above.

KEY CASE: *Wainwright v Secretary of State for the Home Department* [2003] UKHL 53

Background:

A mother and son were subjected to a strip search before being able to visit another son in prison. The Wainwrights were unable to show that what had happened to them was within the terms of an established tort. The HRA was not in force.

Principle established:

The House of Lords was unwilling to develop a new tort of breach of privacy.

The ECtHR, however, held that there was a clear breach of Article 8 (*Wainwright v UK* (2007) 44 EHRR 40).

CONVENTION RIGHTS

Protection of privacy has always been recognised in international human rights. Thus Article 12 of the UN Declaration on Human Rights proposes a right not to be subjected to 'arbitrary interference with . . . privacy' and this is given legal force through an equivalent provision in the International Covenant of Civil and Political Rights (Article 17).

In the European Convention on Human Rights (ECHR) there are two Articles which develop and reinforce the legal protection of privacy.

- Article 8 guarantees the right to 'private and family life, . . . home and . . . correspondence'.
- Article 1 of the First Protocol guarantees a right to 'peaceful enjoyment of possessions'.

Neither of these rights is absolute. They both allow for laws to permit proportionate interferences with private life etc and possessions.

ARTICLE 8 ECHR

A qualified right

Article 8 is a 'qualified' right. It is easy to think of reasons why people should not have an absolute right to their privacy. For example: neglected children may need social workers to interfere in their family life; the media may need to invade a person's privacy in order to expose wrong-doing; public safety may be better secured by deporting foreign convicted criminals even if they have an established family life in the UK; or the prevention of crime may be significantly more effective if the police have access to confidential information or DNA profiles. What is important is that such reasons for interfering with private and family life need to be treated carefully. They should not be allowed to licence interferences that go beyond what is necessary in the context (using legal terminology: interferences must be 'proportionate'). This idea, that the law must seek a balance between the reasons for allowing interference and the need to give proper protection to privacy, is inherent in the structure of Article 8.

Article 8, like Articles 9, 10 and 11, has two paragraphs:

- Article 8(1) establishes the right: 'Everyone has the right to respect for his private and family life, his home and his correspondence'.
- Article 8(2) identifies the exclusive grounds under which laws and state practices can interfere with private life etc.

The definition of 'private life' etc – Article 8(1)

The ECtHR has given a wide definition to 'private life'. It goes far beyond mere privacy, in the narrow, 'inner circle' sense of the term discussed at the beginning of this chapter. In an important case, *Pretty v UK* (2002) 35 EHRR 1, the ECtHR said that 'private life' was a developing concept that could not be exhaustively defined. It included:

- physical and psychological integrity – e.g. treatment by the authorities which leaves a person physicially harmed or psychologically disturbed;
- physical and social identity – e.g. laws which affect, for example, the legal status of children born out of wedlock;
- matters relating to gender, sexuality and sexual behaviour;
- personal development and the ability to develop relations with others – so placing a prisoner in solitary confinement, for example, raises an issue under Article 8;
- personal autonomy. It is not clear what this means. It covers the idea of self-determination – that a person should be free to make the really important choices about their own lives (such as choices about giving birth and dying). But many (including some British judges) have thought it too vague to be a principle of law. It suggests that all restraints on individual's tastes and pursuits are covered – this is going too far (a claim that fox hunting was covered by Article 8 was rejected by a majority of the House of Lords in *R (Countryside Alliance) v AG* [2005] UKHL 52).

Private life also includes:

- Personal information: Article 8 is engaged by the laws and practices by which personal data is protected.
- Reputation: laws by which a person can defend his or her reputation must satisfy Article 8.

The other terms in Article 8(1) are also given wide and inclusive definitions.

- 'Family life' is defined, for example, by reference to settled relationships rather than legal form – so it is not confined to marriage ('family' in Article 8 is given the same meaning as in Article 12 which protects marriage but also the right to 'found a family').
- 'Home' is defined in terms of the place where family life develops and, again, the legal form is insignificant. Thus a trespasser (someone who occupies property without a right to do so) or someone living unlawfully in the country, can still have the right under Article 8 for their home to be respected.
- 'Correspondence' is also defined broadly in a manner that takes into account new methods of communication.

The point to stress is that Article 8 requires states, in their laws and practices, to 'respect' the private and family life, the home and the correspondence that the person already enjoys. It emphatically does not place an obligation on states to provide these things, just not to inhibit their enjoyment or development. Thus Article 8 does not require states to provide homes for the homeless; but to respect the home that a person already has.

Justification – the second paragraph

The mere fact that there has been an interference by a public authority with any of the matters listed above does not mean that there has been a breach of Article 8. The impact of Article 8 is to require such interferences to be justified under the terms of Article 8(2). Whether the justification is sufficient is a matter for a court.

Article 8(2) provides the requirements which must be satisfied if an interference with private life etc is to be justified.

Firstly, any interference has to have proper legal authority – the interference must not only be authorised by domestic law but the content of the domestic law must, in context, mean that interferences are not arbitrary. For example, laws that permit the police to stop and search must be appropriately clear on when and in what circumstances the law can be used and, also, provide proper procedures to safeguard the interests of the person searched (see *Gillan v UK* (2010) 50 EHRR 45).

Secondly, interferences with private life etc must be for one of the purposes listed in the second paragraph, and not for others. Thus, interferences can be justified if they aim, for example, to protect national security, to protect health or morals or to protect 'the rights and freedoms of others'. Noticeably, Article 8 allows interferences with private life if these are in the interests of 'the economic well-being of the country'. Such a provision, which allows a trade-off of basic rights with economic wealth, is unusual in human rights law.

Thirdly, it is not enough to show that an interference with a person's private life etc is based on 'law' and aimed at one of the listed purposes. The particular interference must be 'necessary in a democratic society' – it must be a 'proportionate' way of meeting a pressing social need ('proportionality' has been discussed in Chapter 4). In the context of Article 8 proportionality requires courts to ensure that any particular interference involves a 'fair balance' between, on the one hand:

- the individual's right to private life – which must be given the weight and significance that it ought to have in the context of the interference to that individual;

and, on the other hand,

- the rights of others or the social benefits (such as national security or economic well-being) – which, likewise, must be given the significance they ought to have in terms of justifying interferences with private life etc.

Is Article 8 engaged?	• Does the definition of 'private and family life' cover the facts of the case? • Does the definition of 'home' and 'correspondence' cover the facts of the case?
Has there been an interference with the right?	• Has a law or administrative decision or practice interfered with an Article 8 right? • Has the state's failure to change law or practice and perform its 'positive' duty meant that Article 8 rights have not been protected.
Is the interference 'justified'?	• Is the interference based on 'law' as an autonomous Convention term? • Is the interference for one of the purposes listed in Article 8(2)? • Is the interference a proportionate way of meeting a pressing social need ('necessary in a democratic society')?

Figure 8.1 Summary of the application of Article 8

Positive duties

Often breaches of Article 8 are not based solely, or at all, on an action that a public body has taken or a law passed by Parliament. Rather, the breach stems from a failure to act or legislate. The ECtHR has said, from its earliest cases, that states may have 'positive duties' to ensure that private and family life etc is properly respected. This duty can include ensuring that the people are protected from unjustified interferences not just by the state but also by other individuals or companies. Governments, Parliaments and courts may need to change or apply private law in ways that respect private life. There have, for example, been many disputes, under the HRA, between individuals (often celebrities) and the media who are accused of violating privacy. The media, apart from the BBC, is commercially owned but, nevertheless, can be required by law not to interfere disproportionately with other's privacy. The cases usually involve the courts balancing, in relation to the particular facts, the individual's privacy against the media's right to freedom of expression.

On-the-spot question

Politicians have to accept a more limited right to a private life than the rest of us. Is this good (because we should know about the life and character of those we elect), or bad (because fear of exposure in the media deters decent people from getting into politics)?

The individual and society

Article 8 cases, both in UK courts under the HRA and in Strasbourg, can raise some very difficult issues about the relationship of the individual to state and society. In particular, the concern is how general and public interests can be pursued in ways that adequately recognise and protect the legitimate interests of individuals.

The matter is clearly 'political' in the sense that it involves a critical engagement by the judiciary in decisions and actions taken by the 'executive' (e.g. government ministers, civil servants and other officials) or by Parliament (when the job of the courts is to consider the scope of an Act of Parliament and what actions it does or does not authorise). The issue of 'deference' (which has been discussed in Chapter 4) is important: to what extent is it right for the courts to make up their own mind, on the facts before them, whether the interference is reasonable; or should they 'defer' to the judgment of the public authority or Parliament. For example, the judge might need to consider whether he or she knows enough and is in a position to make a proper assessment of the public interest, and thus give it proper weight against the interest of the individual. Perhaps (though not all commentators agree) it involves the judge giving at least some weight to the fact that Parliament, which enacted the law, was elected by the people or that the ministers who made the decision are accountable to the elected Parliament.

In what follows we look at some examples of the courts struggling with this issue in the context of particular cases.

Environmental law

Convention rights do not include environmental rights, such as a right to clean air and a safe environment. It was not a major issue in the 1950s when the ECHR was drafted. In the modern world it is thought better to have tailor-made treaties, such as the Kyoto Protocol 2005, rather than rely on general statements of human rights.

Nevertheless, in a number of cases the ECtHR has recognised that the enjoyment of the right to private and family life can be drastically interfered with by environmental hazards – such as when the Italian government failed to exercise proper regulatory control over a dangerous chemical factory situated near to a residential area (*Guerra v Italy* (1998) 26 EHRR 357). Where that is the case Article 8 can be involved and the courts must decide whether the interference with private and family life is justified and proportionate.

KEY CASE: *Hatton v UK* (2003) 37 EHRR 28

Background:

Residents living near Heathrow objected to new night flying regulations because the noise was an unjustified interference with their Article 8 rights.

A Grand Chamber, departing from the earlier Chamber judgment, held that there had not been a violation of Article 8.

Principle established:

Article 8 could be breached by noise pollution.

States have a wide margin of appreciation on the matter of airport noise regulation. Many competing economic and social matters have to be taken into account. Night flying could serve the economic interests of the country.

The UK had not exceded the margin of appreciation. The interference was justified and Article 8 not violated.

Unpopular individuals and groups

Article 8 can be the focus of controversy because it can seem to protect the interests of deeply unpopular people.

The deportation of foreign nationals who have committed serious crimes, or of terrorist suspects whose presence in the UK threatens national security, can be halted on the grounds that they have established a family life in the UK which is so strong (especially because of the interests of children) that it outweighs, in the circumstances of the case, the reasons for deportation. The circumstances in which this happens are likely to be rare. An example is *R (H) v Westminster City Magistrates Court* [2012] UKSC 25, where, in one of two cases considered, deportation was halted because of the effects on children.

Individuals who have committed sexual offences can be subject to special, life-time, constraints on their normal life after they have completed their punishment (they are put on the 'sex offenders' register). The Supreme Court, in a decision which 'appalled' the

Prime Minister, found that these people had, under Article 8, a right to a review to ensure that being registered was still necessary. The case was *R (F) v Secretary of State for the Home Department* [2010] UKSC 17 and involved a person who committed serious sexual offences when he was himself a child, and a person who had committed indecent assault as an adult. Without Article 8 they would have been on the register for life with no opportunity to demonstrate that they were no longer a risk.

The fact that a Convention right acts in the interests of the unpopular should not surprise us. One of the main points about human rights is to ensure reasonable treatment for unpopular individuals and minorities who have no way of protecting their interests in a democracy based upon majority rule.

Personal information

One of the areas over which Article 8 has had great impact concerns the use that public authorities, especially the police, make of personal information. If we cannot control the use that others can make of our personal information (e.g. our medical records) then we have no real private life. The protection of personal information is at the heart of Article 8(1). There can be strong public interests in making such information available. In particular it can dramatically enhance the ability of the police to fight crime and bring offenders to justice. Article 8, however, requires the courts to ensure that the laws and practices governing this matter do not involve disproportionate interferences with private and family life.

KEY CASE: *S and Marper v United Kingdom* (2009) 48 EHRR 50

Background:

The Police and Criminal Evidence Act 1984 allowed the police to take and retain DNA samples. As the result of a horrible murder, the law had been extended to enable DNA to be retained even from those who, though arrested, had not then been prosecuted or convicted. The police and Home Office converted the samples into DNA profiles and stored them on a database.

M and S, who had been arrested but neither prosecuted nor convicted, alleged that the storage and potential use of their profiles violated their Article 8 rights.

The ECtHR held that Article 8 had been violated.

Principle established:

Storing DNA profiles for use in the investigation of crime was an interference with the right to private life. Justification for such interference had to be compatible with Article 8(2). This required appropriately detailed and discriminating regulation. To meet these demands of legality and proportionality the regulations covering the database needed to take into account matters such as the age of the persons, whether they had been convicted, the seriousness of the crimes, and so on. This had not happened.

As a result of this case the DNA database was established on a statutory footing (Protection of Freedoms Act 2012) which introduced different rules for children and for the unconvicted etc.

Further applications of Article 8

There are many other areas of life in which Article 8 has had a significant impact. For example:

- rules which discriminate against gays or lesbians are likely to violate Article 8 (although there is no positive duty to permit gay marriage or civil partnerships);
- transgendered persons must not suffer discrimination;
- laws and practices relating to the state's duties on child care, such as adoption, fostering and care orders, have to be administered in ways that are compatible with Article 8;
- tenants of public landlords, can, if there are pressing circumstances, challenge an otherwise lawful possession order (eviction) on the grounds that it is a disproportionate interference with private and family life;
- secret surveillance, though it clearly interferes with a person's private life and 'correspondence', is permissible in order to fight crime and terrorism; however it must be conducted in ways that satisfy Article 8 – there must be proper legal controls and systems of supervision and opportunities for legal challenge;
- abortion. On this controversial matter the Convention provides a wide magin of appreciation. However, women denied an abortion in a morally conservative country, such as Poland or Ireland, can claim that their private life has been interfered with. There is then the issue of justification and countries are allowed to give significant weight to the interests of the foetus and to their underlying culture (see, for instance, *A.B and C v Ireland* (2011) 53 EHRR 13).

PROPERTY – ARTICLE 1 OF THE FIRST PROTOCOL

Introduction – is property a human right

The idea of private and family life is closely linked with the idea of private property. To have proprietorial rights over land, personal property or ideas, is to be legally recognised as the person in control – who can enjoy these things exclusively, decide who else can enjoy them, exploit them economically, sell them or give them to others, or, ultimately, destroy them. Laws of property, in all their complexity, are, therefore, an important means by which a person can insist on being left alone to pursue important parts of their life as they please.

Linking property to privacy can be misleading. Private property is, partly, an expression of the extent to which an individual can lead a private life free of the controls of others. But it is also an expression of economic and social power both private and corporate. It is often asserted by vast, international, commercial corporations and by banks and financial organisations with stupendous economic clout. It can be hard to see why such power and privilege should be able to benefit from human rights legislation. It is because corporate and financial property equates with social power that states seek ways to tax, to regulate, even to nationalise such power in their concept of the public interest. But this is always controversial. On some political views the best way to advance the public interest is by giving private, corporate, economic power as much freedom as possible. It is because of these controversies that the right to the 'protection of property' was not in the original Convention but was added in 1952 by way of the 'First Protocol'. The Convention text that was eventually agreed, Article 1 of the First Protocol, reflects these disputes.

On-the-spot question

Does the legal right to property need to be protected as a 'human right'?

Article 1 of the First Protocol

This right is entitled the 'protection of property' but the term used in the text is 'possessions'. A wide definition has been adopted. It includes not just rights and interests in land and personal property, but also intellectual property rights. Valuable licences, such as permits to sell goods or provide services or rights to practice a profession, also come within the term, as do rights to sue on a contract or in tort. At least some welfare benefits can be treated as possessions. What is not included is a right to aquire property in the future (such as an inheritance); however a legitimate expectation to property (a legally based entitlement to property in the future) may be included.

The legal right to property is divided into three 'rules' – reflecting the three sentences of Article 1.

- First rule (first sentence) – this is a general right to the 'peaceful enjoyment' of 'possessions'. Unlike the other Convention rights, the text makes it clear that this is enjoyed by both 'natural persons' and 'legal persons'. In other words there is nothing to prevent a massive company, with enormous social and economic power, from asserting this right to its property.
- Second rule (second sentence) – this deals with deprivation (taking) of property. People should not be 'deprived' of their possessions except in the 'public interest' and in ways that are in accordance with law and with international law. This can be relevant, for example, when states seek to nationalise industries or compulsorily purchase land.
- Third rule (third sentence) – this deals with controls over the 'use of property' (i.e. short of total deprivation). There is no rule expressed. Rather the text says that the provisions in the first and second sentences 'shall not in any way impair' the rights of states to control the use of property 'in accordance with the general interest'. Rule 3 can be applied in the context of planning and development control, for example.

The text of both Rule 2 and Rule 3 appears to give the authorities very wide powers over the deprivation of property and, in particular, controls over its use. One reading would be that it is almost impossible to challenge in court a deprivation of property or control of its use made by a government so long as it was advancing its conception of the public or general interest. In fact that is not what has happened. The approach of the ECtHR is to apply Rule 2 and Rule 3 in the light of the general requirement found in Rule 1 (the right to peaceful enjoyment of property). In effect this has meant that the courts can adjudicate on whether or not a deprivation or a control of use is 'proportionate' – whether it represents a 'fair balance' between the individual's rights and the rights of others or good of society (the public interests or the general good). This makes Article 1 rather like a qualified right. The focus is on the particular strength of the justification made by the state for its interference with property; and the job of the courts is to assess this with due deference owed to the authorities for their assessment of the public or general interest.

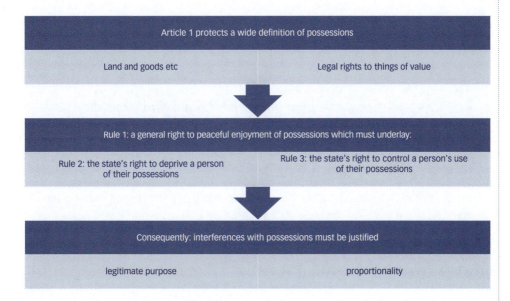

Figure 8.2 Summary of the application of Article 1

But the text of Article 1 is not totally ignored. The references to the 'public' and the 'general' interest require the courts to display considerable deference to Parliament and the executive over the purposes for which property can be taken or its use restricted. Article 1 cannot be used to insist upon 'free market' solutions to all problems. Pursuing social policy objectives by legislation which allows or requires interferences with property rights, is compatible with the Article, so long as it is put into effect in a proportionate way.

KEY CASE: *James v United Kingdom* **(1986) 8 EHRR 123**

Background:

Housing legislation was introduced to give leasehold tenants the right to buy the freehold from the landlord. The Duke of Westminister (the nation's largest landlord) stood to lose significant income from rents. He challenged the law on Article 1 grounds.

The ECtHR held that the legislation did not violate Article 1.

Principle established:

That taking property in pursuit of a social policy (even when it was individuals – here the tenants – rather than the public as a whole who benefited) was not in itself incompatible with Article 1.

This principle has been followed by the UK courts under the HRA in the context, for example, of bank 'nationalisations' responding to the financial crisis of 2007.

KEY CASE: *R (Global Masters) v Treasury Commissioners* [2009] EWCA Civ 788

Background:

Northern Rock, a bank, collapsed and was taken into public ownership. Shareholders objected to the low valuation given to the shares.

The Court of Appeal found there was no violation of Article 1.

Principle established:

Article 1 would only be violated if property was taken in pursuit of a policy that had no rational basis. Nationalisation of Northern Rock was a rational exercise of social and economic policy.

Breaches of Article 1 characteristically involve deprivations or restrictions on the use of property which are done in a way that is disproportionate or undermines some important principle of the rule of law. For instance:

- Chronic procedural delay in dealing with planning applications (*Sporrong and Lönnroth v Sweden* (1983) 5 EHRR 35).
- Preventing a successful litigant from putting into effect a court judgment and an award of damages by a retrospective change to the law (*Pressos Compania Naviera v Belgium* (1996) 21 EHRR 301).
- Taking property through compulsory purchase with inadequate compensation (*Scordino v Italy* (2007) 45 EHRR 7).

SUMMARY

Article 8 and Article 1 of the First Protocol aim to guaranteee that individuals (and sometimes companies) should have areas of their lives which are immune from the interference of others, including, but not only, the state. As we have seen, as legal rights these are both very flexible. They allow legitimate interference by the authorities when this serves a democratic government's conception of the public good and when the impact on the individual is proportionate.

ISSUES TO THINK ABOUT FURTHER

Technology gives the state massive capabilities to access the population's internet and other electronic communications. For what purposes this should be done, and the extent to which it can be properly controlled and regulated in ways that protect private life, is a major legal issue for the near future.

FURTHER READING

- Lester, Pannick and Herbage, *Human Rights Law and Practice*, 3rd edn, 2009, Lexis-Nexis (available online).
  Chapter 4, Article 8 offers a comprehensive account of Article 8 with references to both Strasbourg and UK cases.
- Wacks, R., *Privacy, A Very Short Introduction*, 2010, Oxford: OUP.
  This book discusses the general arguments about privacy and wonders, at the end, whether technology will bring about its death.
- Çoban, A.R., *Protection of Property Rights within the European Convention on Human Rights*, 2004, London: Ashgate Publishing.
  This book contains a full discussion of the concept of property within the ECHR as well as seeking a fuller theoretical framework for the law's development.

COMPANION WEBSITE

Additional content from the author is available on the companion website:
www.routledge.com/cw/beginningthelaw

Chapter 9
Freedom of political expression

LEARNING OBJECTIVES

On completing this chapter the reader should understand:

- The importance of political rights as guaranteeing more than just the right to vote
- The need for legitimate restrictions on the exercise of such rights
- The general structure of Articles 10 and 11 in respect of guaranteeing rights of political expression and protest
- Applications of these rights in the context of the media and in relation to expression which undermines democracy.

INTRODUCTION

The right to participate in public affairs is important and easily explained by reference to human rights theory and justifications. People should be entitled to take part in the processes by which the policies to be pursued by government and the means to be used are decided; and also to be involved in public affairs more generally. In this way people can advance their personal interests by obtaining changes to the law and state policy, but also express a more 'ideal regarding' interest in making society better for everyone. In a democracy this is done, predominantly, by the right to vote for representatives (such as MPs) in regular, fair, elections (guaranteed by Article 3 of the First Protocol to the ECHR). It is also done by securing rights to express opinions and hear the opinions of others etc, and to be able to organise into groups, such as political parties, and to march, hold meetings and demonstrate in order to influence public opinion and the representatives and then the government.

In this chapter we look at how these rights of public participation are guaranteed in human rights law, especially through Articles 10 (freedom of expression) and 11 (freedom of assembly and association) of the European Convention on Human Rights (ECHR), given effect in UK law through the Human Rights Act 1998 (HRA).

The philosophical justification for these rights, especially freedom of speech and expression, is not confined to public or political speech. Wider, more fundamental, human interests are served by freedom of expression. These include:

- the never ending pursuit of truth,
- the nurturing of individual autonomy and the value of consciousness and choice,

- the maintenance of a society which is dynamic, always developing and not being stultified, and
- empowerment of a population against would-be dictators seeking to control access to ideas and information.

Individual autonomy and social dynamism, both served by freedom of expression, require a democratic political system in which people can know about, and contribute to, the conduct of public affairs. A definition of 'democracy' that excluded freedom of expression, assembly and association would be peculiar. Freedom of expression (and association and assembly too) has many forms and purposes, all of which fall within the protection of human rights law, but that protection is at its strongest in respect of political expression. This term is broadly defined to include not just political matters in the narrow sense of pertaining to government but to all 'questions of public interest' (*Wingrove v UK* (1996) 24 EHRR 1, para 58). It is easier for states to justify restrictions on purely commercial or artistic expression, assembly and association than it is to justify such restrictions in respect of public matters.

On-the-spot question

 What are the main justifications for freedom of expression; which do you think are most important (consider Lord Slynn's account in *R v Secretary of State for the Home Department ex p Simms* [2000] 2 AC 115, page 126 f–h)?

Qualified rights

A moment of reflection on these freedoms (expression, association and assembly) shows that their exercise can have a significant impact on the rights and freedoms of others. Others may be offended, their reputations reduced, their confidential information made public or their right to a fair trial undermined by things said and done by people exercising these freedoms. Likewise, there may be important common and social interests that need to be protected: the protection of defence and national security secrets are obvious examples. It follows that reasonable restrictions on these freedoms are desirable, even necessary, and can be perfectly consistent with a well-functioning democratic society. What is controversial is the specific detail of the principles justifying such restrictions and also over their application in particular situations and circumstances. An example of the first would be a principled disagreement on whether expression which is merely offensive but does not otherwise affect people's ability to live their life as they choose, could justify a criminal sanction. An example of the second would be that there is widespread agreement that speech can be suppressed to protect national security but, equally, disagreement as to whether the content of a particular article, book or film is sufficient to justify suppression.

Legal approaches

Legal approaches to protecting freedom of expression differ.

The First Amendment to the US Constitution (that Congress shall make 'no law' abridging freedom of speech, the press, peaceful assembly or the right to petition the government) appears to make little, if any, concession to the rights of others or public interests that might be harmed by speech or assembly. Even so there have been, and remain, different theories about its meaning and application. At times (such as around the First World War and during the McCarthy period) it failed to prevent the enforcement of laws which penalised anti-war sentiments and the advocacy of socialism and communism. By the second half of the twentieth century, however, it had been transformed, by the Supreme Court, into a means of defending speech, no matter how offensive or seditious, which does not involve a direct incitement to violence.

In England the traditional approach was that everyone had the right to say etc whatever they wanted, subject to whatever constraints the law imposed. 'The law' in this sense meant the common law administered by a judiciary which was independent of the executive and which could and did provide remedies against the executive if it acted outside the law. The common law, for example, allowed for the protection of reputation through a civil action for defamation (libel and slander). The judges asserted an often reactionary conception of the common good and state interests in common law crimes of 'seditious libel' (roughly: for attacks on the state and the constitutional order) and 'blasphemous libel' (attacks on established religion). Parliament, of course, could and does abolish or amend the common law or introduce new laws. Seditious and blasphemous libel were both abolished in 2008, for example, and the Defamation Act 2013 makes major amendments to libel and slander. Acts of Parliament can also introduce new restrictions which are unknown to the common law, such as, in the twentieth century, laws dealing with official secrets, public order, racial hatred and terrorism.

Human rights

The problem with this traditional approach was that it placed most emphasis on the rights of those seeking to restrict the speech of others. The rights of the speakers have no particular significance or weight over and above the default position – the liberty to speak unless limited by these interests that the law protects. Lacking, under this approach, was a positive entitlement to speak or otherwise express oneself which had to be respected unless overwhelmed by other interests. Such an entitlement gives the speaker a basic legal status as a rights-carrier. This status has then to be recognised by the courts and given due weight against the claims of those seeking to restrict speech. To be fair, by the last decades of the twentieth century there was express recognition of a fundamental right to freedom of expression inherent in the common law (see, for instance, *Derbyshire County Council v*

Times Newspapers [1993] AC 534). But it was not until the ECHR was given further effect in UK law under the Human Rights Act 1998 that positive rights were clearly, with Parliamentary authority, made part of the law.

CONVENTION RIGHTS: ARTICLES 10 AND 11

Given that there are reasonable grounds for restricting speech, assembly and association, these are qualified rights. The first paragraph of each Article defines the general freedom which states are to guarantee; the second paragraph identifies the exclusive basis on which freedom of expression, assembly and association can be restricted.

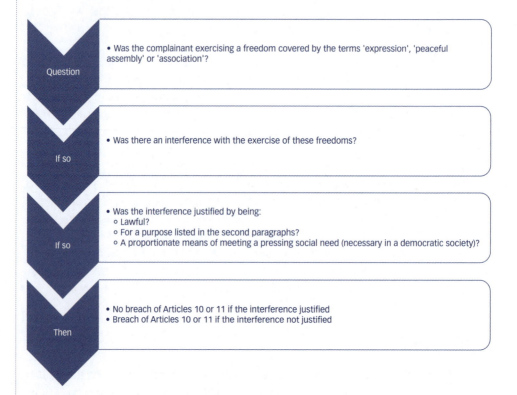

Figure 9.1 The general process of dealing with a case under Articles 10 or 11

The scope of Article 10(1) and Article 11(1)

Article 10(1) guarantees a right to 'freedom of expression'.

- 'Expression' is given a wide definition. It includes not just speech but all other forms of expression such as writing, musical composition, singing, photography, painting etc. The sloganising and other forms of display that may be part of a political demonstration can also engage Article 10(1), and so restrictions on demonstrations can be dealt with under Article 10 as much as under Article 11, depending on the context.

- The purpose of the expression is normally irrelevant and includes political, commercial and artistic expression etc.
- As well as the right to 'hold opinions' and 'impart' ideas and information, the first paragraph of Article 10 protects the right to 'receive' ideas and information. This is potentially very important since most people do not have much opportunity to speak in a public forum but do have a strong interest, as citizens, in being well-informed on public matters. However, this provision, by itself, is of limited use since the ECtHR has said that it cannot generally be used against an unwilling provider (*Leander v* Sweden (1987) 9 EHRR 433) (unless needed to protect some other right, such as the proper respect for private life). There is evidence that the ECtHR is changing its position and now looks more favourably on the rights of 'watchdogs' (e.g. the media or some NGOs) to compel the disclosure of public information (*Tarsasaga a Szabadsagjogokert v Hungary* (2011) 53 EHRR 3).

Article 11 guarantees 'freedom of peaceful assembly' and 'freedom of association'.

- 'Assembly' refers to meetings, marches, demonstrations etc and 'association' to forming, joining and participating in clubs, societies, political parties, churches etc.
- The definition of 'peaceful' assembly can be problematic. Does it include demonstrations that are non-violent but obstruct others (it often does); does a person lose his or her rights if, with peaceful intentions, they participate in a demonstration that, because of the actions of others, turns violent (they do not)?
- Article 11(1) also protects the right to 'form and join trade unions'. Interesting questions of interpretation arise as to whether this includes the right not to join, or to leave a trade union, a matter of some importance if (as used to be the case in Britain) there is a 'closed shop' which makes union membership a condition of employment.

Case study: Police tactics

The effectiveness of rights to protest and demonstrate can depend on police tactics. Complaints of over-reactions by the police are common. In exercising their powers, such as preventing breaches of the peace, police must act in a lawful and proportionate manner.

KEY CASE: *Austin v Metropolitan Police Commissioner (MPC)* [2009] UKHL 5

Background:

Police 'kettled' May Day demonstrators – they contained them at Oxford Circus for many hours before being released. The police aim was to distinguish between the peaceful and the violent. The legal question was whether this was a 'deprivation of liberty' (under Article 5 ECHR) and therefore actionable in the courts as a 'false imprisonment'.

Principle established:

There could be no 'deprivation of liberty' in the context of proportionate actions taken by the police in good faith to control a political demonstration.

KEY CASE: *Moos v MPC* [2012] EWCA Civ 12

Background:

During the G20 protest of 2009 there were two groupings of demonstrators – one 'peaceful' the other 'violent'. The peaceful camp was 'kettled' in order to avoid contamination by the violent camp.

Principle established:

The *Austin* principles were applied. The police action in the circumstances was proportionate and in good faith.

Has there been an interference?

Usually the answer to the question whether or not there has been an interference, by the authorities, with persons' rights to expression, assembly or association, is obvious – there is a law which authorises or requires a restriction or there has been an act by a minister, local council or official of some kind which prevents or limits expression, assembly or association. Where issues of interpretation can arise is if a restriction on a person's freedom is imposed not by the state but by another private person or by a company, such as an employer restricting the free speech rights of its employees. A court may then have to decide whether the state, the government and the legislature retains responsibility so that Articles 10 or 11 impose a positive duty to change the law in order to protect freedom of expression or association in these circumstances.

Legitimate interference

If there is an interference with the exercise of these freedoms protected by Articles 10 or 11, the focus is then on whether the interference is justified. Justification must be in terms of the second paragraph, Articles 10(2) and 11(2) and the burden of proving justification is on the state.

1. Interferences must be lawful.

   As discussed in Chapter 4, this means that interferences must not only be allowed by the domestic law, but the domestic law must also meet the Convention standards of being accessible, foreseeable and non-arbitrary. Where, for example, the police have over-broad discretion in the context of a political demonstration so that it is hard to predict when powers may be used or there is little, effective, legal control (and so no legally enforceable protection against arbitrary actions), there may be a violation of Article 11.

2. Interferences must only be to achieve one of the purposes listed in the second paragraph.

   Purposes for which expression, assembly and association can be restricted:

   - the interests of national security and public safety,
   - preventing disorder or crime,
   - protecting health or morals, and
   - protecting the rights and freedoms of others.

   Purposes for which, additionally, only expression can be restricted:

   - territorial integrity,
   - protecting reputations and confidentiality, and
   - maintaining the authority and independence of the judiciary.

On-the-spot question

 Allocate an area of English law which serves each of the purposes for which freedom of expression and assembly can be restricted (e.g. 'defamation' restricts speech in order to protect reputation).

3. Proportionality.

    Showing that an interference with expression, assembly or association serves one of the legitimate purposes listed in the second paragraphs of Articles 10 and 11 is relatively easy for the state. The real disputes and controversies on these matters tend to be on the third issue of justification: is the interference 'necessary in a democratic society'?

    A court must decide whether the interference is a proportionate way of meeting a pressing social need. This usually involves judges balancing:

    (a) the degree and nature of the burden imposed on the applicant's freedom with
    (b) the significance of the rights of others which may be affected or the general good of society (see Chapter 4 for general discussion of these terms).

    It is at this point that the heavy weighting given to expression and assembly on public affairs comes into play. Thus, to restrict someone's 'political' expression in order to protect the rights of others is likely to be justified only if the expression would attack the essence, the core point, of the other's threatened right (e.g. that a criminal defendant would not otherwise receive a fair trial; or that proper confidentiality would be lost if publication went ahead).

Political speech

The central roles that these political freedoms, of expression, assembly and association, play in a democracy mean that only the most compelling reasons can justify restricting the activities of elected politicians.

KEY CASE: *Castells v Spain* (1992) 14 EHRR 445

Background:

The ECtHR held that Article 10 was breached when a member of the Cortez (Spanish Parliament) was prosecuted for insulting the government.

Principle established:

Political speech enjoyed the highest protection under the ECHR.

Political organisation

Likewise, political parties and other associations must be free to organise and take part in activities. This extends even to parties with radical views, pursuing their aims against a background of political violence.

KEY CASE: *United Communist Party v Turkey* (1998) 26 EHRR 121

Background:

The banning by the Turkish authorities of the UCP violated Article 11. The party was banned because of its constitutional aims, not because of anything it did.

Principle established:

Whilst a political party's activities may, perhaps, justify suppression, its participation in and promotion of a cause the state disapproves of does not.

Enforcing 'morality'

The right to 'hold opinions' in Article 10 means that state harassment of persons (e.g. banning, prosecuting etc) merely because of their opinions, especially on public matters, breaches Article 10. An important feature of this is that Article 10(1) protects expressions which 'shock, offend and disturb' and Article 11, likewise, protects assembly and association even though the elected government or the majority of the population are repelled by the cause being promoted. There is no point in a right to freedom of expression if it is merely the right to say popular things.

Some writers (famously Lord Devlin exploring the case for the 'enforcement of morality') have argued that social cohesion depends upon some general moral values. Expression which is wholly inconsistent with these values can be penalised. The original target in the 1960s was homosexual law reform, but it has re-surfaced in various areas such as anti-racism, pornography, anti-westernism and religious dress.

The position under Article 10 is not altogether clear. The general thrust of the Convention is based on a liberal perspective which would protect speech etc that does not harm others in the sense of not damaging their interests and ability to live their life as they please. On the other hand, Article 10(2) does accept that proportionate interferences with expression can be for 'the protection of morals'. On issues such as control of pornography, the Court accepts a wide margin of appreciation thus leaving it mainly to states to decide what moral standards should apply with its own role being supervisory. Restrictions of speech which offends on racial or religious grounds may be justified as being for the protection of the 'rights of others'. The Convention text does not specify what those 'rights of others' are. The ECtHR has accepted that they can include rights not to be gratuitously insulted on religious or racial grounds. If the other tests of legality and need are passed, such restrictions can be compatible with Article 10.

THE MEDIA

It is vital in a democratic society that there is a vigorous and free media. This is fully recognised by the courts, including the ECtHR. The role of the media is:

- to make information on public matters available so that citizens can make their choices, and also
- to be a 'watchdog' acting as a constant check on the behaviour of government and public bodies.

But the media can overstep the mark. They may, for example, publish stories which invade a person's privacy, say something about a defendant prejudicial to the fairness of his or her trial, write a story in such a way that it encourages violence or publish information that really threatens national security.

'Duties and responsibilities'

Article 10(2) (but not Article 11(2)) asserts that the exercise of freedom of expression 'carries with it duties and responsibilities'. Such a requirement of responsibility can be the basis of laws which restrict media freedom in ways that are compatible with Article 10. In the UK, for instance, journalists may be able to avoid liability for otherwise defamatory stories (the stories enjoy 'privilege'), but only if the journalism is 'responsible'. Of course, there needs to be care: 'responsibility' can, at the hands of the national authorities, be a basis for restrictions on speech which only serve the interests of those in power. The 'duties and responsibilities' cannot be used to prevent vigorous, critical, disrespectful, radical and oppositional forms of expression.

Protection of sources

In order to fulfil their 'watchdog' role effectively, journalists need to be able to protect the anonymity of their sources. This can mean, though, that those harmed by a disclosure may be unable to obtain an adequate remedy. An example would be a celebrity patient whose medical records are disclosed when an anonymous nurse leaks them to a journalist. Under the Contempt of Court Act 1981, s 10, the journalist cannot be ordered to disclose the source unless factors, such as the rights of others or the interests of national security, require this. The ECtHR has stressed the importance of guaranteeing journalistic freedom in this context and has, in some cases, given greater weight to this than was given by the judges in the UK.

RESTRICTIONS: PRIVATE RIGHTS

Political expression, association and assembly can interfere with the 'rights of others'. A demonstration, for example, can involve trespassing or an interference with the rights of others to use the highway. In the context of expression the commonest issue is where some speech or writing seriously undermines a person's reputation. If so, a person can bring an action for what is called in English law 'defamation' (libel or slander).

There is a clear danger that this can have what is called a 'chilling' effect on free speech, especially when done by the rich and powerful. In one famous case (*Steel and Morris v United Kingdom* (2005) 41 EHRR 22) the vast McDonalds food chain sued two impoverished political activists for what they had said in a pamphlet about health, environmental and other issues. McDonalds won on some counts, lost on others, but the activists endured huge disruption to their lives, though they clearly 'won' as regards publicity.

Seeking the proportionate 'fair balance' required by Article 10(1) and 10(2) requires a legal framework which allows protection for free speech whilst recognising the legitimate rights of individuals to protect their reputations. The law should distinguish between comment (which should not be restrained) and untrue factual assertions which damage reputation. The English defence of 'fair comment' embodies this idea. This distinction of facts and comment is, in practice, difficult to make. In *Lindon v France* (2008) 46 EHRR 35 the ECtHR upheld a defamation case brought against a French publisher who claimed to have published a novel. The central character was obviously based on a prominent right wing politician, who was presented as a racist.

Restriction: public interests

Public interests, not just private rights, can also be reasons for restricting freedom of expression. In particular, the government may think it proper to use the law to prevent speech and other expressive acts which it believes threaten national security. This may involve the criminal law: in the UK it is a crime under the Official Secrets Act 1989 for unauthorised disclosures of information concerning national security to be made.

More significantly, the civil law can be used. The government may go to court for a civil injunction to prevent, for instance, a newspaper publishing a story it believes threatens national security. Such injunctions involve 'prior restraint': the government's aim is to prevent the story ever being published. The courts grant such injunctions to protect confidentiality because the whole point of confidentiality would be lost if publication was permitted – damages are inadequate. But because they prevent publication at all, the state has a heavy burden of justification to discharge. Section 12 HRA requires judges to ensure they give full weight to freedom of expression when deciding cases.

Such claims, and the principles on which free speech injunctions could be issued, underlay the 'Spycatcher' saga which gripped the nation in the 1980s.

KEY CASE: *Observer and Guardian Newspapers v United Kingdom* **(1991) 14 EHRR 153**

Background:

Mrs Thatcher's government tried to prevent newspaper serialisation of *Spycatcher*, a book by Peter Wright a one-time intelligence officer. The book dealt with his experiences, some of which suggested unlawful actions by the secret service. The government sought an injunction based on protecting confidentiality in respect of both specific information which disclosure might be damaging and also knowledge of the general workings of the security services. Initially successful, in the end (this was a *cause celebre* lasting a number of years) the government lost both in the domestic courts (the House of Lords eventually refused a full injunction) and the ECtHR.

Principle established:

The government could, compatibly with Article 10, use the ordinary civil law in order to protect not only particular information which disclosure would be damaging but also the secrecy of the secret services generally. However, such restraints on free expression had to be justified under Article 10(2). Once confidentiality was lost, as a matter of fact, continuing with an injunction was, because futile, disproportionate. This had occurred once *Spycatcher* was published in the USA. Continuing the injunctions beyond then breached the Article 10 rights of the newspapers.

Limits to protected expression, assembly and association

As the discussion above shows, most of the case law on Articles 10 and 11 involves weighing the rights of expression, association and assembly against public interests and the rights and interests of others that can be legitimately protected in a democratic society. But there are some ways of exercising these political freedoms that take a person or organisation outside the protection of human rights law altogether and which cannot be tolerated even in a pluralist and democratic society committed to human rights.

In issue is a long-standing dilemma of liberal thinking: to what extent is intolerance to be tolerated?

- One view is that there is very little that should not be tolerated in respect of political expression, organisation and assembly. The exercise of such freedom, properly understood, involves providing reasons for action which the rest of us are free to assess and only follow if we make our own judgement that the ideas proposed are worth following. If a person or organisation advocates breaking the law they are not responsible if laws are broken by others who, as autonomous beings, have chosen to accept and act on the reasons given.
- Militant democracy. Others find the radical disjunction between giving reasons for action and acting for those reasons unrealistic. So a second view, sometimes called 'militant democracy', is to accept that the exercise of some political freedom can be suppressed in the name of protecting democratic institutions and processes.

A strong, though controversial, tendency towards 'militant democracy' can be found in the European case law. It is usually based on the approach to justification under the second paragraphs. As mentioned above, racist speech and other forms of bigotry can be suppressed in order to protect the 'rights of others'. A hugely controversial example was the ECtHR's upholding, under Article 11, of the ban on a leading, victorious, Islamist party in Turkey. This was on the basis that, if it was to form the government, the party might introduce Sharia'h to Turkey (*Refah Partisi v Turkey* (2003) 37 EHRR 1). 'Militant democracy' is also based on Article 17 ECHR. This Article says that human rights cannot be used to enable any activity aimed at the 'destruction of the rights of others'. It has been used, for example, to allow the banning of parties which might introduce totalitarian regimes and the suppression of what, in the view of the Court, is morally worthless speech, such as denial of the holocaust (which is based on the denial of established facts) or Islamaphobia and other forms of bigotry.

On-the-spot question

 Is it right to have crimes which are committed by speech or action which offends, shocks or disturbs but is not harmful in other ways? Consider also the 'enforcement of morals', discussed above.

Incitements to violence ('go out and kill') can be suppressed compatibly with human rights so long as the words used, the form in which they are uttered and the context shows a sufficiently close, causal connection with acts of violence. The Council of Europe requires states to make 'public provocation' of terrorism a crime. The resulting UK offence involves 'encouragement' of terrorism by means which include the 'glorification' of past or future events. Serious doubt has been expressed (e.g. by the Parliamentary Joint Committee on Human Rights) as to whether this offence can be enforced compatibly with Article 10.

SUMMARY

Articles 10 and 11 provide a legal framework for the control of political speech, assembly and association. They require any restraints of these freedoms to be fully and properly justified.

ISSUES TO THINK ABOUT FURTHER

Social media (Twitter etc) can be an extremely effective means by which people express their political opinions and mount campaigns. But it can also be a vehicle for vile extremism and anonymous, destructive, abuse. The pressure to regulate is already mounting. The difficult question is how this can be done compatibly with human rights.

FURTHER READING

- Schauer, F., *Freedom of Speech: A Philosophical Inquiry*, 1982, Cambridge: CUP (esp Part 1). This book provides a full discussion of the philosophical justification of freedom of speech.
- Thornton, P., *The Law of Public Order and Protest*, 2010, Oxford: OUP. A comprehensive discussion of public order law in the UK; Chapter 10 deals specifically with human rights.
- Barendt, E., *Freedom of Speech*, 2nd edn, 2005, Oxford: OUP. An authoritative consideration of legal and political issues relating to freedom of speech in different contexts.
- Harvey, P., 'Militant Democracy and the European Convention on Human Rights', *E.L. Rev.* 2004, 29(3), 407–20. An interesting discussion of the ECtHR's approach to the issue of tolerance of the intolerant.

COMPANION WEBSITE

Additional content from the author is available on the companion website: www.routledge.com/cw/beginningthelaw

Chapter 10
Freedom of belief

LEARNING OBJECTIVES

On completing this chapter the reader should understand:

- Why the law recognises beliefs as being important enough to be protected as a human right
- The nature of the two absolute rights (to hold beliefs etc and to change one's religion) that are guaranteed by Article 9(1)
- The nature of the qualified right protected by Article 9(1) – the right to 'manifest' a belief
- The grounds on which the state can restrict manifestations of belief (Article 9(2))
- That freedom of belief is also protected by the duty of states to respect parental beliefs in the education system (Article 2 of the First Protocol)
- The importance of Article 9, under the Human Rights Act, for equality law in the United Kingdom.

INTRODUCTION: IMPORTANCE OF BELIEF IN MODERN SOCIETY

Human rights law has always tried to protect the right of people to have deep convictions, religious or otherwise, and to live their lives accordingly. The UN Declaration of Human Rights, the International Covenant on Civil and Political Rights and Article 9 of the European Convention on Human Rights (ECHR) guarantee 'freedom of thought, conscience and religion' and 'beliefs'.

'Beliefs', religious or non-religious, imply something more fundamental than mere 'opinions' (the right to hold opinions is protected by freedom of expression – Article 10). A belief engages with matters which are deep and profound and important to the interests of mankind. Furthermore, beliefs are likely to have some form of more-or-less organised expression – through a church (through which beliefs may be authoritatively expressed) or in terms of a looser structure such as a movement or a community which, although looser, still provides an external point of reference for the believer.

'Thought and conscience' describe matters which are more subjective. A matter of conscience relates to what is of decisive importance to an individual's own sense of his or her integrity and dignity; a matter of conscience does not necessarily (though it may) invoke a collective or public sense of what is right or wrong.

The European Court of Human Rights (ECtHR) has frequently expressed the importance of belief. Article 9 is 'in its religious dimension, one of the most vital elements that go to make up the identity of believers and their conception of life, but it is also a precious asset for atheists, agnostics, sceptics and the unconcerned' (*Bayatyan v Armenia*, app Grand Chamber judgment of 7 July 2011).

Modern capitalist societies, including Britain, value diversity and multi-culturalism. These values represent the positive reaction to a long, disfiguring history of discrimination. Significant movements of population in the last 50 years mean that these societies must accommodate and treat fairly and justly, different social groups – many of which are defined by their religious faith.

But it is vital not to assume that the human right to thought and conscience is somehow confined to religious belief. Atheistic beliefs, coupled with the sense that all the great metaphysical questions can be sufficiently answered through science, may be held with an equivalent seriousness. Likewise there are a range of secular concerns, from the environment to vegetarianism, that people treat with great moral seriousness and which clearly have the character of beliefs.

CONVENTION RIGHTS

Under the Human Rights Act 1998, statutes, such as the Equality Act 2010 (discussed at the end of this chapter), must be interpreted for compatibility with Convention rights; and public authorities (such as local councils) and courts and tribunals must, likewise, act in ways that protect Convention rights. In this context there are two principal rights:

- Article 9 provides a right to 'freedom of thought, conscience and religion'. This is, partly, a qualified right. Therefore (as we have seen with Article 8 and Articles 10 and 11 in earlier chapters) the right can be interfered with so long as the interference is done lawfully, for a legitimate purpose and proportionately (any interference must be 'necessary in a democratic society').
- Article 2 of the First Protocol concerns education. It guarantees a right of children to benefit from the education system of the country. It also confers a right on parents to have their children educated in a manner consistent with their beliefs. As we shall see, the way this right is drafted and interpreted means that parents do not have an absolute right to veto or exempt their children from all educational policies.

ARTICLE 9

Article 9 guarantees three particular rights.

1 The right to hold religious beliefs

This is an absolute right. The state cannot impose beliefs upon people. The state cannot require a particular religion or form of worship and make it a criminal offence not to conform. Likewise, the civil law should not give preferences or impose disadvantages on adherants of religious or other beliefs. For example, laws under which associations are to be registered and allowed charitable or other status, cannot be based on the superiority of one set of beliefs over another; nor can refusal to register be based upon a bad faith concern with procedural irregularities.

The importance of this position cannot be exaggerated; it goes to the very heart and centre of the consciousness of the 'modern' European world as it emerged from the religious wars and turmoil following the Reformation. In pre-modern Europe a person could be burnt for his or her beliefs and wars of appalling ferocity, such as the Thirty Years War in Germany 1618–1648, were motivated by a desire to compel beliefs onto the population of a state. In the 'modern' world religion is re-cast as a private matter of individual belief and conscience. A state must be secular or neutral.

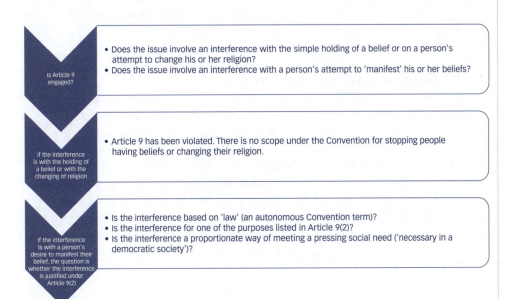

Is Article 9 engaged?
- Does the issue involve an interference with the simple holding of a belief or on a person's attempt to change his or her religion?
- Does the issue involve an interference with a person's attempt to 'manifest' his or her beliefs?

If the interference is with the holding of a belief or with the changing of religion
- Article 9 has been violated. There is no scope under the Convention for stopping people having beliefs or changing their religion.

If the interference is with a person's desire to manifest their belief, the question is whether the interference is justified under Article 9(2)
- Is the interference based on 'law' (an autonomous Convention term)?
- Is the interference for one of the purposes listed in Article 9(2)?
- Is the interference a proportionate way of meeting a pressing social need ('necessary in a democratic society')?

Figure 10.1 Summary of the application of Article 9

A secular state is one, like Turkey, whose institutions are deliberately designed not to reflect any particular religion and where religion or faith is allowed no presence in parliament, courts, universities, etc. Such a state can flourish even amongst a religious society and population.

A neutral state can be one which allows faith and religion a visible place in its institutions; but, at the same time, allows all other faiths, and those with no faith, to participate fully as equals in the political, social and economic life of the nation. The United Kingdom is an example. The Church of England is established by law with the monarch at its head. At the same time there is full equality for all: no religious 'tests' are imposed upon civil servants or army officers and civil and political equality is enjoyed irrespective of belief. In effect the law is neutral as between different beliefs. On this basis, the existence of an established church is not a violation of Article 9.

2. Right to change religion

Article 9 includes the right to change religion.

This right sits comfortably with the idea that the state must be neutral as to the truth of a religious belief because belief is fundamentally a deeply private matter. It is less easy to deal with in an Islamic state where 'apostasy' (abandoning one's religious faith) can be taken as an insult to God and can, in principle and according to some traditions, be punished with death. Given the secular nature of the state in Turkey, this has not been a direct issue under Article 9. However, the fact that an organisation aims to impose this view of Islamic law on apostates may be a reason why banning it does not violate Article 9 (as in *Kasymakhunov v Russia*, app 26261/05 judgment of 14 March 2013).

3. The right to manifest a belief

Article 9 also guarantees a right to 'manifest' a religion or belief 'in worship, teaching, practice and observance'. This is the area that has created most case law and issues.

A manifestation of a belief is the idea that a belief may be so important to an individual that he or she is driven to 'bear witness to the belief in words or deeds'. For example, believers may limit their diet (such as the eating of only kosher foods by some Jews), or wear particular clothes (such as the wearing of headscarves by some Muslim women) or wearing jewellery (such as a Kara worn by some Sikh women or a crucifix worn by some Christians). Manifestations of belief can also involve conscientious refusals to perform what would otherwise be a duty.

Manifestation of belief needs to be contrasted with actions that are merely motivated by belief but do not have that intimate connection that is required for 'manifestation'. Article 9 does not gurantee a right to behave in a manner governed by one's beliefs, especially in relation to public life and public duties. So, for example, the courts are not sympathetic to claims, based on Article 9, by Quaker pacifists that they should be allowed to redirect a portion of their tax into a special fund that cannot be used for military purposes (*R (Boughton) v Her Majesty's Treasury* [2005] EWHC 1914).

People who manifest their beliefs can interfere with the rights and freedoms of others. Actions taken for conscientious reasons may damage the interests of others. Manifestations of belief may be seen as symbolic attacks on social values taken seriously by the majority or (which is a different thing) may seem to undermine hard won principles of a liberal society. Religions may impose requirements of behaviour and dress on adherants, especially women, which seem inconsistent with liberal equality and which employers may reject as poor role models. Parents may seek to insist that their children are educated in ways that seem to narrow rather than broaden their children's minds. People may seek, on conscientious grounds, exemption from what would otherwise be their legal duty or may seek to prevent others doing things which the law allows. As a result, Article 9 allows domestic law to interfere with manifestations of belief.

Justifying interferences with manifestations of belief

Article 9 allows such interferences with manifestations of belief (not with the holding of beliefs), but only if these interferences are justified by reference to Article 9(2). What must be justified are either the particular laws or administrative practices that directly authorise interference, or laws (such as employment laws) that allow private persons, such as commercial employers, to interfere with people's manifestations of their beliefs. As with other qualified rights (Articles 8, 10 and 11) the interference, if it is to be justified, must meet the requirements of the second paragraph (Article 9(2)). The interference must:

- Be authorised on a sound legal foundation – the rules of domestic law must allow it and, furthermore, the relevant provisions of domestic law must meet the Convention requirement that the application of the law can be foreseen with reasonable certainty and its application is not arbitrary.
- Be only for one of the purposes listed in Article 9. These include protecting 'health or morals' (which could be relevant in the context of religious dietary rules) and also 'the rights and freedoms of others'.
- Be 'necessary in a democratic society'. The interference must be dealing with a significant social problem ('a pressing social need') and the particular actions in question must be a proportionate way of meeting this need. This involves a close examination by the court of the issues in the case and the justification given. The court seeks a 'fair balance' between the need to deal with the problem and the impact of the individual's actions.

A good example from English law is *Begum*.

KEY CASE: *R (Begum) v Governors of Denbigh High School* [2006] UKHL 15

Background:

B, a schoolgirl with Muslim beliefs, insisted, for religious reasons, on wearing a more concealing form of dress than was permitted under the school rules. The question was whether her exclusion from school violated her right to freedom of belief under Article 9.

Principle established:

- B was, indeed, asserting her right to freedom of belief. The school's uniform policy and her consequent exclusion from education were an interference with this right. Therefore the question for the court was whether this interference was justified.
- The interference was based on clear and accessible school rules and policies and so was prescribed by law.
- The interference was aimed at protecting the rights and freedoms of other Muslim girls at school who might otherwise be subject to external pressure to wear clothes they did not want to wear.
- The measure, as applied to B, was proportionate. The school's uniform policy had been carefully drawn up, following consultation with Muslim leaders, and represented a fair balance of factors. The House of Lords had no basis on which it could superimpose its own judgment onto that of the school.

The substance of beliefs

The protection of the manifestation of beliefs, as a matter of human rights, is subject to another important but difficult constraint. The ECtHR, followed by UK courts, requires the belief being manifested to meet a 'certain level of cogency, seriousness, cohesion and importance'. For the religious this test is likely to be met by membership of a church or adherence to the tenets of a recognised religion.

Religion is inclusively defined and not confined to the five 'great' religions (Budhism, Christianity, Hinduism, Islam and Judaism) and their different denominations. Courts have had little difficulty, for instance, in holding that Druids and Rastafarians hold 'religious' beliefs (*Arthur Pendragon v United Kingdom* App. 31416/96 Commission admissibility decision of 19th October 1998 and *R v Taylor* [2001] EWCA Civ 2263). But there are limits and it has been suggested (in *Grainger*, see below p. 151) that the religion of the 'Jedi Knights' may fail the seriousness and cogency tests (despite the fact the 2011 census indicated 176,632 adherents). More problematic are non-religious beliefs which may be very personal and particular. Judges, who must embody state neutrality, are understandably reluctant to examine for credibility the tenets of a belief.

Attention is likely to focus on beliefs that invoke hostility to others. The ECtHR has made it clear that 'beliefs' with manifestation protected by Article 9 must be worthy of respect in a democratic society and not involve conflicts with the rights of others. Racist 'beliefs', no matter if held sincerely, are likely to fall outside the protection of Article 9. More problematic are beliefs which are associated with leading religions which, in at least some versions, are inconsistent with human rights – some conceptions of Sharia'h exemplify this (see *Refah Partisi v Turkey* (2003) 37 EHRR 1, an Article 11 case, discussed in Chapter 9).

In any event, proponents of such beliefs may be prevented by Article 17 from pursuing their Article 9 claims. Article 17 prevents people from using their rights in order to undermine the rights of others. Both Article 17 and the justification for interference under Article 9(2) must be used with care. There is little point in protecting beliefs if they can be set aside too easily. Societies that are committed to human rights have to accept that people may hold and manifest beliefs that the majority (or those in social, economic and political power) find vile, disgusting and threatening.

On-the-spot question

?
How comfortable are you with the idea that a judge should be required to evaluate the coherence and legitimacy of someone's beliefs? Consider why it was that Lord Walker found the idea 'alarming' in *R (Williamson) v Secretary of State for Education and Employment* [2005] UKHL 15 (para 60); do you agree with him?

Conscientious objection

Conscientious objection has often arisen in the context of people seeking to avoid compulsory military service ('conscription'). This may be because they have general pacifist convictions or because they disapprove of some particular military action they would be involved in. In the past the ECtHR refused to read into Article 9 a right of conscientious objection in this context. This was because Article 4 (the right not to be enslaved or made to undergo 'forced labour') expressly exempted compulsory military service. Lately this has changed – probably reflecting the fact that few European countries make their young people undergo military service any longer (other forms of social service may be required). Now conscientious objection to military service will be within Article 9(1) and so the issue, in any particular case, turns on whether action taken against such a person can be justified (*Bayatyan v Armenia* (2012) 54 EHRR 15).

Conscientious objection can often pit the individual's interests against the interests of others, or the common good as identified by those in power in a democratic country. Conscientious objection should be tolerated but toleration can be limited if, for example, it means that the rights of others are undermined, or important public services can no longer be made available on equal terms to all.

KEY CASE: *Eweida and others v United Kingdom* (2013) 57 EHRR 8

The background:

E worked on the check-in desks for British Airways (BA). She insisted, as an expression of her Christianity, on wearing a visible cross whilst working. This was contrary to company policy at the time and she was suspended without pay.

C was a nurse who was banned from wearing a cross whilst on duty.

L was a registrar of births, deaths and marriages who lost her job when she refused to perform civil partnership ceremonies since she believed that same-sex unions are contrary to God's will.

M was a marriage guidance counsellor who refused, on religious grounds, to give sex counselling to same-sex couples.

Principle established:

E & C: wearing of a cross was a manifestation of their beliefs and so protected by Article 9(1).

- In E's case the ECtHR found that there was very little interference with the rights of others (the uniform policy was changed and E reinstated). BA is a private company, so the issue was whether the UK's positive obligation to secure E's right to manifest her beliefs was properly secured by UK employment law. The ECtHR found there was a violation. There was no problem about the domestic law which required UK courts to rule on the proportionality (the overall balance of interests) of the ban. On the facts, however, the ECtHR simply took a different view from the Court of Appeal of the proportionality of BA's actions.

- C was also manifesting her religious belief. However, here, the employer was a public authority. Its dress code was driven by needs for health and safety. In deciding the 'fair balance' question the authorities had to be given a wide margin of appreciation. There was no violation.
- L and M were both manifesting their beliefs. However in both cases their employer had strong policy justifications in terms of providing services to all on conditions of equality. Article 9 was not violated.

On-the-spot question

Do you agree with the decisions on C, L and M in *Eweida* or do you think, in effect, that they allow laws and employers supported by those laws, to trample over people's genuine conscientious objections?

ARTICLE 2 OF THE FIRST PROTOCOL (ARTICLE 2)

Freedom of belief also comes up in the context of the right to education. The question of a right to education was controversial and so its introduction into the Convention was delayed and put into the First Protocol. It is controversial, first, because of the role of the state. In totalitarian societies party-dominated states seek to indoctrinate school children with a particular ideology which they will carry with them all their lives. On the other hand, the state has a vital role in providing education to the majority of the population who could not otherwise afford it. Secondly, education is a 'social' right which distinguishes it from most of the civil and political rights in the Convention. Social rights often require expensive positive actions (such as the provision of free schooling) which states may be unwilling to commit themselves to as a legally enforceable obligation.

Equal access to the education system

Given these concerns, it is no surprise that Article 2 does not provide a direct right to education. Rather it is a right to equal access to the education system that is provided. The leading Strasbourg case, for example, is concerned with the rights of parents to have their children educated in their native tongue (*Belgian Linguistic Case (no 2)* (1979–80) 1 EHRR 252). Cases in the UK under the Human Rights Act 1998 have been concerned, for example, with school exclusions.

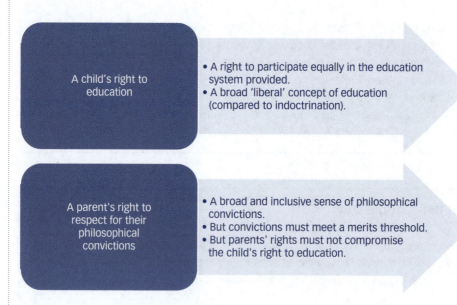

Figure 10.2 Summary of the application of Article 2 of the First Protocol

Education and parental philosophical convictions

The second right in Article 2 is most relevant to this chapter. Article 2 assumes that parents have the 'right' to have their children educated in 'conformity with their own religious and philosophical convictions'. Presumably this right is based upon the natural affinity of parents and children. Article 2 insists that the state must 'respect' this right. 'Respect' is a less absolute requirement than 'guaranteee' or 'ensure', for instance. However, it does involve something more than merely 'taking into account' and may impose on states positive obligations to make adjustments in order to secure parental interests.

There is a tension between the liberalism that is inherent within the Convention and this right of parents. Education is to do with equipping the individual with the knowledge and skills needed for a full and fruitful life. Liberalism stresses autonomy and a fruitful life is one in which the individual can choose for him or herself what is important, valuable and worthwhile. Such choices can only be made if education is open and gives students a range of experiences. Parents, on the other hand, may want to insist that their children's education is confined to certain things that they, the parents, hold to be true.

As ever, it is a balance that needs to be struck. From earliest cases, such as *Belgian Linguistics*, the ECtHR has insisted that these parental rights must not contradict the right to education in the first sentence. It follows that there is a 'quality' threshold that parental 'convictions' must cross. These issues were discussed in the following case.

KEY CASE: *Campbell and Cosans v United Kingdom* (1982) 4 EHRR 293

Background:

Parents, who objected to corporal punishment, were unable to obtain assurances from the Scottish education authorities that corporal punishment would not be used against their children.

The ECtHR held that deeply held views on school punishments could be 'philosophical beliefs'; and that the Scottish education authorities had failed to respect these beliefs. There was a breach of Article 2 of the First Protocol.

Principles established:

- Convictions: like 'beliefs' (Article 9), 'convictions' are more profound than mere opinions (protected by Article 10). They must 'attain a certain level of cogency, seriousness, cohesion and importance'.
- Religious: as with Article 9, 'religious' has an inclusive meaning and is not confined to the tenets of the great religions.
- 'Philosophical' is not confined to systems of thought, but refers to views on important matters so long as they are 'worthy of respect in a democratic society', not 'incompatible with human dignity' and are consistent with the 'fundamental right of the child to education'.

It is not enough just to show that parents are acting on the basis of their religious or philosophical 'convictions'. There is also the need to balance the weight of these convictions against other values, in particular the child's right to an education and the reasonableness of the policies pursued by the state in respect of that right. *Campbell and Cosans* can be compared with *R (Williamson) v Secretary of State for Education and Employment* [2005] UKHL 15, a case decided under the HRA. Here a group of parents and teachers of children at independent Christian schools objected to the total ban on corporal punishment imposed by Act of Parliament. The House of Lords accepted that the parents were acting on the basis of their 'religious convictions' but found that there was no failure of 'respect' for these convictions. It was reasonable, in educational terms, for parental views to be overridden in this context (the ban was also justified under Article 9(2)).

Parents may also find that their religious or philosophical convictions are challenged by elements of the school curriculum such as sex or religious education. The same principles apply: the convictions must cross the quality threshold and the state must ensure that it at least 'respects' these convictions. In order to 'respect' parental convictions, the state must ensure that it educates and does not indoctrinate. The curriculum needs to be taught with a degree of openness and flexibility and it needs to be reasonably impartial and not doctrinaire – as the ECtHR said in *Kjeldsen, Busk, Madsen and Pedersen v Denmark* (1979–80) 1 EHRR 711 (a sex education case) knowledge and ideas must be conveyed in an 'objective, critical and pluralistic' manner.

Article 2 does not, however, require absolute neutrality on all things. This might be philosophically impossible (in the sense that no curriculum could ever be neutral, judgements on what is valuable always have to be made) but also might require education authorities to ignore the traditions and culture that are valued, or taken for granted, by majorities in any particular society. States have a wide but not unlimited margin of appreciation (defined in Chapter 4) on these matters. As always it is a question of a court seeking a proper balance between maintaining important features of tradition and culture and ensuring that these are not imposed in an overly doctrinaire manner. In *Folgero v Norway* (2008) 46 EHRR 47, for instance, the ECtHR held that the importance given to Christianity in a compulsory religious studies course was too much and tended towards indoctrination; in *Lautsi v Italy* (2010) 50 EHRR 42, on the other hand, it was held that having a crucifix in the classrooms of Italy was within the margin of appreciation and had no influence on the curriculum.

EQUALITY LAW

As well as directly involving human rights, the protection of 'thought and conscience' and 'belief' concerns equality law (also discussed in Chapter 4). This important area of law has developed in recent years. The grounds of discrimination have been extended beyond the original concerns with race and sex to include other categories such as disability and sexual orientation. These 'protected categories' (as they are called in UK law) now include 'religion and belief'. Furthermore, modern equality law is not just concerned with the avoidance of discrimination but extends to a broader idea of ensuring equal opportunity. This may require steps to be taken to remove barriers to participation that people in the protected categories can experience. Often important decisions involving the right to freedom of thought, conscience and belief are taken in the context of equality law.

KEY CASE: *Grainger v Nicholson* **[2010] ICR 360**

Background:

N had been appointed Head of Sustainablility to a large property investment company. He thought their policies were inconsistent with his views on climate change and he made consequent disclosures which he believed were the real reason for his dismissal. The company said they had made him redundant. For procedural reasons he could only challenge his dismissal if he could prove discrimination on grounds of philosophical belief. The preliminary issue was whether views on climate change could be a 'philosophical belief' and so protected by equality regulations (if they were thought to be merely political ideas, they would not have protected status under English law).

The Employment Appeals Tribunal held that Grainger's views on climate change, if sincerely held, were capable of being philosophical beliefs protected from discriminatory actions.

Principle established:

The equality regulations (see now the Equality Act 2010) should be read in the light of Article 9 ECHR (a Convention right under the HRA 1998).

To be protected by discrimination law a belief had to satisfy various tests of importance, coherence and seriousness and also to be compatible with a democratic society and human rights.

A protected belief did not need to be religious, it could be based upon science.

In order to be protected by discrimination law a belief had to be sincerely held. In this case there needed to be evidence of sincerity on which the applicant should be cross examined.

On-the-spot question

? Do you think *Grainger* draws the line correctly between political opinions (which are not protected by Article 9) and 'philosophical convictions' (which are)? Note that discrimination in the way Convention rights are applied, which is based on political convictions, may violate Article 14 (see Chapter 4).

SUMMARY

The right to thought, conscience and belief is fundamental to human well-being. At the same time people who insist on acting according to their beliefs can impose significant burdens on others and challenge beliefs and values that others, perhaps the majority, hold dear. The job of the courts is, as so often in human rights law, to work towards a fair balance and thereby ensure that societies remain open, tolerant and pluralist.

ISSUES TO THINK ABOUT FURTHER

For many decades in the post-war world, the dominant character of public debate was secular. This has now changed. Faith communities are being more assertive, it seems, but are being challenged by the claims of scientific atheism and feel themselves challenged by the secular indifference of equality law. Human rights law is likely to be a forum in which these fierce arguments take place.

FURTHER READING

- Harris, D.J., O'Boyle, M. and Warbrick, C. *Law of the European Convention on Human Rights*, 2009, Oxford: OUP.
  Chapters 10 and 23 contain comprehensive explorations of Article 9 and Article 2 of Protocol One, respectively, in terms of the law and decisions of the ECtHR.
- Lester, Pannick and Herberg, *Human Rights Law and Practice*, 2009, London: Butterworths (carried on Lexis®Library), Chapter 4, Article 9 and Article 2 of Protocol One.
  These chapters offer a comprehensive account of the UK and Strasbourg law as it applies to both these articles.
- Ahdar, R. and Leigh, F., *Religious Freedom in the Liberal State*, 2005, Oxford: OUP.
  This book upholds the importance of belief and religious faith.

COMPANION WEBSITE

Additional content from the author is available on the companion website:
www.routledge.com/cw/beginningthelaw

Index

Please note that page references to Figures will be in *italic* print. 'ECHR' stands for 'European Convention on Human Rights', while 'ECtHR' represents 'European Court of Human Rights'.